# Projecting Possibilities for Writers

## for Writers

### The How, What & W
### of Designing Units of Stu

**K–5**

# MATT GLOVER & MARY ALICE BERRY

HEINEMANN
Portsmouth, NH

**Heinemann**
361 Hanover Street
Portsmouth, NH 03801–3912
www.heinemann.com

*Offices and agents throughout the world*

**Library of Congress Cataloging-in-Publication Data**
Glover, Matt.
    Projecting possibilities for writers : the how, what, and why of designing units of study, K–5 / Matt Glover and Mary Alice Berry.
        p. cm.
    Includes bibliographical references.
    ISBN-13: 978-0-325-04192-6
    ISBN-10: 0-325-04192-X
    1. English language—Composition and exercises—Study and teaching (Elementary).   I. Berry, Mary Alice.   II. Title.
    LB1576.G477 2012
    372.62'3—dc23                                                    2012025263

*Editor:* Zoë Ryder White
*Production:* Patty Adams
*Cover photographer:* David Kominz
*Cover and interior designs:* Monica Ann Crigler
*Typesetter:* Gina Poirier Design
*Manufacturing:* Steve Bernier

Printed in the United States of America on acid-free paper
16  15  14          ML      2   3   4   5

**To Harrison, for all of the stories**
**—MG**

**In memory of my mother, Mary Lee Ball**
**and for Darryl, always and forever**
**—MAB**

# Contents

# Acknowledgments

*Each of us has cause to think with deep gratitude of those who
have lighted the flame within us.*

*—Albert Schweitzer*

You would think this would be the easiest section of a book to write. How hard can it be to say thank you to all those who have helped you? But it is hard. It is hard because there is no adequate way to express our deep gratitude to everyone who supported us and was responsive to our needs throughout the development and writing of this book. Please know how much we value all of you and wish we had a better way to say thanks.

This book would not have been possible without the infinite patience of our editor, Zoë Ryder White. Zoë feels like more of a coauthor than an editor. Her expertise in supporting young writers and the craft of writing greatly influenced both the content and quality of the writing. Thank you, Zoë, for answering our countless emails, gently questioning our thinking, and nudging us to completion.

Many others at Heinemann have helped us on this journey. Kate Montgomery supported the idea for this book from the beginning and encouraged us to share the work we had been doing with a wider audience. We greatly value her ongoing support. Margaret LaRaia provided feedback early on that helped direct our thinking, as did the rest of the wonderful editorial team at Heinemann.

We are Katie Wood Ray fans. She has profoundly impacted our thinking about teaching ever since we were first lucky enough to work with her many years ago. This book wouldn't have been possible without Katie's landmark book *Study Driven*. Thank you, Katie, for helping us think through the big ideas.

We have the great fortune to belong to a professional learning community of wonderful consultants led by Ellin Keene and Vicki Boyd. We want to let them know how much we appreciate the important conversations focused on what is important for children.

Of course, we could not have written this book without the help of fellow teacher researchers and learners. Many colleagues from Lakota Local Schools have helped us clarify our thinking. Thank you to Asha Ruiz and Kaelin Harrison, who provided insights into their process for projecting units of study and for meeting with us so early in the morning.

We also thank the members of Lakota Literacy VIEW Committee and the staff of Shawnee Early Childhood School for your support.

We have had the great opportunity to work with and learn from teachers across the country and internationally. We'd like to thank each school we've planned units with. We started to list them all (more than fifty) but we're afraid we'd miss one. So if we've used this projection process with you, thank you for helping us refine our thinking.

Others have contributed to the book by sharing their reflections and samples of their students' work. Thank you to everyone who graciously sent us writing, including Mary Baldwin, Lisa Cocoran, Sue Culverhouse, Nancy Hagerty, Theresa Haler, Ben Hart, April Hilton, Pegeen Jensen, Colleen Leach, Teddi Longardt, Diane Newman, Eve Robertson, Asha Ruiz, Laurie Smilack, and Jen Thiel. Matt would especially like to thank Jan Reckley from Lawrence Township for helping him *immerse* so many teachers in units of study.

Peggy Banet, Pat Mascaritolo, and Diane Keene continually remind us with their examples that children are the center of the work we all do. Thank you to Kathy Collins for always having the perfect analogy, and to Mary Baldwin for her infectious enthusiasm.

Matt would like to thank his children, Harrison, Meredith, Molly, and Natalie, for allowing him to use stories from their lives to illustrate important ideas. He's never at a loss for a new story. And of course he wants to thank his wife, Bridget, an amazing natural teacher, who helps Matt see stories he might otherwise miss.

Mary Alice thanks her mother—her first and still her best teacher. She must also say thank you to her students for their inspiration and for reminding her of the wonder in the world around us. Most importantly, she thanks her husband, Darryl, for his love, support, and laughter, and for surrounding her with all things beautiful.

# Introduction

*Teachers—like children and everyone else—feel the need to grow in their competencies; they want to transform experiences into thoughts, thoughts into reflections, and reflections into new thoughts and new actions. They also feel a need to make predictions, to try things out, and to interpret them . . . Teachers must learn to interpret ongoing processes rather than wait to evaluate results.*

—Loris Malaguzzi

Teaching is the act of making hundreds of decisions each day, and when we are well prepared, we make better decisions. In our professional development work, teachers often ask us about decisions related to teaching writing, especially those teachers who have recently started using a writing workshop in their classrooms. They've become comfortable with the structure of whole-group teaching during minilessons and share/reflection time. They're having writing conferences with students and are starting to feel more confident in identifying student strengths and relevant teaching points. But, about a month or so in, teachers new to workshop teaching often start wondering, "What do I do next? I have a writing workshop launched and students are writing independently, but *what should I teach?*" Daily minilessons are based on what they see students doing, but they wonder, where is this teaching going?

Of course, there are also veteran teachers who are shifting their pedagogy, teachers who have more experience with the material but want to experiment with a more student-driven classroom and curriculum. They ask questions like "How do I modify my current curriculum to allow room for adjustments?" and "How do I balance goals with flexibility in my daily or monthly plan?" We propose that answers to these questions can be discovered when teachers think through, or *project*, how a unit of study in a writing workshop could unfold.

The process for designing (or "projecting") units of study described in this book grew out of our work with teachers in our school, and continued to be changed and refined as we worked with teachers in a diverse range of school and educational environments. We have worked together for over fifteen years, much of that time at a large early-childhood school just north of Cincinnati. Matt was the principal and Mary Alice was everything from literacy coach to media specialist to gifted teacher. Matt is now a full-time author and consultant, working with preschool through sixth-grade teachers across the country and internationally in the area of writing. Mary Alice is currently teaching first grade and conducts work-shops for teachers in preschool through sixth grade focused on writing.

## How This Book Works

Our goal is to provide practical support for teachers to create a unit of study in writing workshop, so much of the book focuses on this process. But before we describe the process we need to examine the rationale behind projecting a unit of study. There-fore, Chapter 1 looks at the importance of responsive teaching, while Chapter 2 looks at the importance of organizing your teaching into units of study and how projecting a unit prepares you to support your young writers. Chapter 3 provides a brief over-view of the projecting process, allowing you to see the entire progression from start to finish. Then, Chapters 4 to 8 examine each step in greater depth. We hope that as you read this book you will go through the process with us, so that by the end of the book, you have projected your own unit of study for use in your classroom.

As part of our goal to make this process easy to use, Chapters 4–8 conclude with two sections:

- **Projecting Mary Alice's Unit of Study:** We wanted to provide a vision of how projecting a unit could unfold with an actual teacher and an actual unit, so in these sections we listen in on Mary Alice and her colleagues as they project a unit called Realistic Fiction. It's important to note that our goal in sharing this unit is to focus on the process, not on the genre of realistic fiction. These sections also describe how a realistic fiction unit would be projected in an intermediate-grade class.

- **Try It Out:** Each chapter ends with a section that leads you step-by-step through the process of projecting your own unit of study, regardless of which unit you decide to create.

We aim for these two sections to put the in-depth thinking into the context of an actual unit and make the entire process easier to replicate.

## A Process That Supports All Teachers

While we were working on this book, Matt and our editor, Zoë, met to talk about the project. As often happens, they tried to strike a balance between what they were sup-posed to talk about (getting some work done on the book) and what they wanted to talk about (all sorts of issues related to teaching and children). During one of their many tangents, they started talking about their experiences as new first-grade teachers. Matt reflected on how too much of his teaching had a "fly by the seat of your pants" feel to it. It wasn't that he didn't plan or know where his teaching was going. But he didn't feel his teaching was as powerful as it could have been. He knew that the teacher's guides he had been given didn't reflect the needs he was seeing in his students, and that he wanted to create his own pathways to better support his class. He made adjustments as best he could. He knew what he didn't want to do (follow a guide) and what he wanted to do (create his own plan), but he wasn't sure how to do it. He lacked a process.

Zoë's experience was different. While there were plenty of seat-of-the-pants moments, planning a writing curriculum generally led to a day-by-day plan rather than a flexible projection. Zoë enjoyed the benefit of pooling resources and planning with smart colleagues, but the process led to identical units. Zoë could have used these unit plans as flexible projections, but as a teacher new to the grade, she wasn't sure how—and generally ended up following them explicitly, sometimes leading to a disconnect between her teaching and the actual kids.

Mary Alice's experience was different still. When Mary Alice was a student teacher, planning simply meant writing page numbers in a plan book. Monday, pages 24–27; Tuesday, pages 27–32, and so on. She couldn't wait to get her own classroom so she didn't have to teach this way. But when she was hired for her first teaching position, she was given no curriculum or teaching guides. In some ways this was what she had hoped for, certainly better than just following guides page by page. Yet it was overwhelming, and she constantly questioned whether she was teaching her students everything she should. Many years later, Mary Alice is now back in the classroom and benefits from years of working with amazing educators. She is now better able to find a balance between overly prescribed instruction and seat-of-your-pants teaching, by creating learning experiences based on standards, district curriculum, best practice, and the current needs of her students.

Matt's, Zoë's, and Mary Alice's experiences as teachers mirror what we see in classrooms across the country: teachers who want to create their own units but aren't sure how. Teachers who feel they must follow a set of plans or units laid out by someone else. Teachers who plan learning experiences based on standards but strive to keep their teaching flexible and responsive. And increasingly, it seems, teachers who feel they are less and less empowered to make decisions based on what happens in their individual classrooms each day. Our hope for this book is to support all of these teachers by showing a process for creating units that fosters teaching and learning that is more meaningful, powerful, and lasting.

# Responsive Teaching in the Writing Workshop

When Matt's son Harrison was very young and just starting to talk, he often answered questions with the phrase "I can't know." Not, "I *don't* know" but "I *can't* know." For example, if Matt said, "Why did you pour your juice on the dog?" Harrison would look at Matt and in all sincerity say, "I can't know." He meant to say "don't know," but it came out as "can't know." It was as if he were saying, "Gosh dad, I'd like to help you out with that question, but since I'm only three I can't possibly begin to know why I did that. It's beyond my comprehension. I *can't* know."

Over the years, Matt and his wife Bridget would often use the phrase "I can't know." When the refrigerator broke, Bridget asked Matt where they were going to get the money for a new refrigerator, and Matt half jokingly said, "I can't know." Since it was early in their marriage and money was tight, it was a question beyond his comprehension. As Matt shared this story with Mary Alice and other colleagues at school, the phrase "I can't know" stuck and would pop up whenever difficult questions arose.

Of course, Harrison's answer was more a result of his early language development than a true articulation of the difference between "can't know" and "don't know." But the idea expressed by "I can't know" is significant, especially when it comes to creating meaningful and engaging learning experiences for students.

If you say "I don't know" you are implying that you could have an answer, but you don't know it right now. The answer is knowable. But "I can't know" is something very different; you're stating the answer is unknowable. You don't know the answer, and neither does anyone else. You *can't* know.

The concept of "I can't know" is important when deciding what to teach in any instructional area, and is particularly crucial when creating writing workshop units of study. When you create a unit of study, it's tempting to think you know exactly what will happen on day five or thirteen or eighteen of a unit of study. But, in reality, you *can't* know what will happen on day thirteen until you and your students live the twelve days that come before it. In fact, the only way you can know what will happen on day thirteen is if you decide to ignore students for the first twelve days and teach by strictly adhering to a plan, blind to what is happening in your class each day.

Anyone who has taught knows the many reasons daily flexibility is necessary. The smallest things can throw your day off track, anything from a child getting sick to a spider suddenly deciding to crawl across your meeting area. You have to know when it is best to regroup and move on or when you should capture the moment (or the spider) and let the excitement and energy lead you in a new direction. Since you can't know what will happen, you have to be ready for the unexpected. If this is true for any single day, then it's also true during a well-thought-out unit of study in writing workshop.

Great teachers have always responded to what their students need by making adjustments. They watch and listen closely to see the impact of their teaching, and then adjust their teaching accordingly. Responsive teachers don't cover material; they teach students. We can't know for sure what will happen on each day of a study, even if we have each day planned. As soon as a unit starts, we begin making adjustments based on the many ways our students respond to our teaching. Our goal for this book is to provide teachers with a process for projecting a unit of study that empowers them to make effective decisions as they respond to the students they work with each day.

## Why Make Adjustments Within a Unit of Study?

Here are some reasons teachers might decide to make changes over the course of a unit. (We'll see some examples of how unit adjustments play out as a unit unfolds in Chapter 8.)

- **Students need more time to grasp a concept.** You thought your third graders would be able to quickly plan headings for their feature articles, but then you realized they needed additional support in creating a clear organizational structure.

- **Students are engaged with a topic and need more time.** In a unit of study on punctuation, your first graders become fascinated with their discovery of the multiple ways that authors get their readers to pause, and you decide to go with this interest for a few extra days.

- **Students already know the skill you planned to introduce.** You were planning to spend several days on similes and metaphors with your fourth graders in a poetry unit, but you quickly discover that they remember them well from third grade and can apply them in their poems, so you move on to another topic after one day.

- **Students want to try out a new skill you had not anticipated.** You weren't planning on teaching your kindergartners about the illustration technique of zooming in and zooming out as part of your illustration study, but after they notice it in a mentor text and want to try it, you decide to include this technique in your unit.

- **Students need a skill or concept earlier than you had initially planned.** You were planning on waiting until later in your personal essay unit to teach your sixth-grade students that their thesis statement doesn't have to be in the first paragraph. But, you decide that it would make more sense to teach this when they plan their essay.

- **Only a small group of students needs help with a certain skill.** You were anticipating teaching your second graders how to punctuate dialogue as part of your unit on realistic fiction, but you discover that only four students need support with this, so you pull them together in a small-group conference to practice.

## The Difference Between Projecting and Planning

In this book, we intentionally use the word *projecting* instead of *planning*. The word *planning* subtly implies that you know what you will teach throughout the unit. A plan tells you

### CHILDREN'S QUESTIONS GUIDE OUR TEACHING

In the writing workshop, individual writing conferences are models of responsive teaching, because most conferences start with the teachers asking questions of the student. Asking a child a question puts her in a powerful position. After the child talks, the teacher must then craft a response. In writing conferences, we don't know exactly what we are going to teach until the child starts talking. We can't know for sure what the child is going to say, so to teach well we need to listen carefully and respond to what the child says. This is true at the unit level as well.

what you will do each day. As Katie Wood Ray says in an email message, "Plans are actions you set out to do. Projections are what you imagine might happen" (Ray 2011).

The word *projection* communicates how you imagine a unit might unfold. It's your best guess of what will happen if everything goes exactly as planned during the unit. And of course, at least in our experience as teachers, nothing ever goes exactly as expected, especially when you're thinking about several weeks' worth of teaching. The word *projecting* captures the spirit of thinking ahead and being prepared without closing the door on opportunities to make adjustments. Projecting a unit implies not knowing for sure what will happen (you can't know!), yet being prepared for the many possible ways a unit might unfold.

Here's another way to look at the difference between a plan and a projection. The educators in Reggio Emilia, Italy, use the term *progettazione* for all flexible planning (Edwards 1998). Carlina Rinaldi, one of the profound educators in Reggio Emilia says, "I like to use the metaphor of taking a journey, where one finds the way using a compass rather than taking a train with its fixed routes and schedules" (p. 119). Carlina's metaphor makes us think of the difference between following Mapquest directions and using a road map. Mapquest directions tell you exactly how long your trip will take and what time you will arrive at each city along the route—like a unit that is planned day by day before it begins. A map, on the other hand, provides endless possibilities for how to reach the same destination. When you use a map you *project* how you will get to your destination, but you can choose between multiple routes and make adjustments as you go. You can stay longer in a town that interests you, or zip through a town if there's not much to see. You can take detours down side roads, and then get on a highway if you want to make up time—and you'll have a clear sense of where you are and how far you are from your destination the whole way.

Teaching with a road map rather than a set of Mapquest directions allows for the complexity of the responsive classroom: the best route for one child may be different from the best route for another. Projecting is crucial when creating learning experiences for entire classes that also work for individual students with different needs. We can start by having a good sense of our destination—where we want to be and what we want students to be able to do at the end of the unit—and we'll absolutely need a map, a *projection*, that provides countless ways of getting there.

## Roadblocks to Responsive Teaching

Barriers that reduce teachers' power to make decisions have negative effects on teachers as well as students. As Tom Newkirk states, "When teachers lose control of decision making—when they prepare students for tests they have no role in designing (and often no belief in), when they must abandon units they love because there is no longer time, when they must follow the plans designed by others, when they are locked into systems of instruction and evaluation they don't create or even choose—they will not be relieved of stress. Their jobs are not made easier, they are made harder and more stressful. While some find a way to resist, others acquiesce, though they feel, as one teacher put it, that 'the joy of teaching is being drained out of teaching'" (Newkirk 2009, pp. 24–25).

The loss of control that Tom describes also eliminates responsive teaching, the kind we know works best for students. We're not advocating a teaching environment where each teacher decides on her own standards and curriculum. But we believe teachers can and should make decisions within the broader context of curriculum and standards based on their students' needs, on a daily basis. In our work with teachers in school districts across the country, we have experienced several barriers that can inhibit teachers' freedom to project possibilities for units of study and make decisions based on what they see. You may have experienced some of these barriers:

- **Writing programs provide a daily script of lessons.** By design, writing programs lend themselves to being used as a plan, rather than as a projection. Some of these programs are designed to provide a set schedule of daily lessons to be taught regardless of what's actually happening in the classroom. These programs are written for children in general. The authors *can't know* the specifics of your current class. In our experience, the idea that all students need the same thing at the same time on the same day doesn't fit with how children learn and grow. There are also some unit resources that were designed for use in projecting units, but are often misused as a day-by-day script. This leads to the unintended consequence of decreasing teacher decision making and responsiveness.

- **District and/or school administrations believe all classes learn at the same pace.** School administrations sometimes inhibit teacher thinking and decision making in their well-meaning attempt to ensure that all students receive the same high-quality education. Some school districts expect that all teachers across a grade will be teaching the same lesson on the same day. We can't imagine a less responsive teaching environment than one where teachers aren't able to make decisions based on the needs of the students.

At the school where Matt and Mary Alice worked together, all of the kindergarten classes were half-day sessions. Each kindergarten teacher had one class in the morning, and one in the afternoon. We didn't expect the morning class and the afternoon class to be at the same point in a unit on the same day. Anyone who has ever taught two half-day kindergarten classes knows how different one class can be from the other. If two different groups of students, with the *same* teacher, are in different places in a unit, how could we possibly expect five different groups of students with five different teachers making decisions, to be in the same place at the same time? This is true as well in higher grades that are departmentalized. A sixth-grade teacher with five different math classes expects each class to need different amounts of support to understand different concepts. The goals would be the same but the path for getting there would be different.

- **Teachers doubt their ability to teach their students responsively.** We occasionally hear teachers say, "Just tell me what to teach and I'll teach it." We know that teachers are as varied as their students and therefore have different styles and comfort levels. In a world of increasing pressure on educators, teachers want to make sure they're doing the *right* thing.

Not being comfortable with the content you are teaching also leads to relying on outside resources. If Mary Alice suddenly had to teach seventh-grade math, she wouldn't feel confident teaching that content. She would need some practice to learn how to tell whether or not her students were on track. It's likely that she would be more dependent on a teaching guide at first. Many of us were not taught to write the way our students are being taught. If your only experience with writing was to write about an assigned topic or to follow a template, then you would be taking a risk to step away from what you know. You may be unsure about how to help students generate topics or try out different ways to organize their writing. Following someone else's plan might feel safer, but ultimately someone else's plan can't meet the needs of your students as well as you can.

◆ ◆ ◆

Fortunately, these barriers don't have to stand in the way of responsive teaching. Teaching should be a joyful endeavor, for both teachers and students. We aim to show teachers how they can project units of study that allow for responsive decisions based on what is happening in their class each day within a context of high expectations and standards, regardless of whether or not the roadblocks we've described are present.

# Organizing Your Teaching into Units of Study

During a recent conversation about teaching, our friend Kathy Collins described units of study as a beautiful necklace of beads. Individual beads are beautiful to look at and hold in your hand, but a bead doesn't do much on its own. When individual beads are connected with a chain, they become something more powerful. Their colors and textures play off of each other and they create a stronger sense of a whole entity. They work together to create a necklace that is more beautiful than all of the beads individually.

The analogy of a necklace works particularly well as we think about units of study in writing workshop because just as beads can be moved, changed, and rearranged to improve the quality of a necklace, minilessons within a unit can also be changed and altered to create a more effective unit of study. When it comes to designing learning experiences for students in the form of units of study, all teachers need to be able to make decisions regarding which minilessons (and in what order) will lead to more effective learning. This book is designed to provide you with processes and tools to become like jewelry designers as you project units of study.

The process this book describes will help you make the types of responsive teaching decisions discussed in Chapter 1. These decisions assume that you are organizing your writing workshop instruction across the year into units. That sounds obvious, but the decision to organize writing instruction into units is an important one. Before we delve into the actual process of projecting units, let's look at the importance of organizing writing instruction this way and what types of units you might consider.

# Why Units of Study Matter

The key word in the phrase *unit of study* is *study*. The implication is that students will engage in inquiry, in studying a stack of relevant mentor texts that the teacher has gathered (and studied herself) for the unit. (See Chapter 5 for an extensive look at stacks of mentor texts and how to use them.)

There are numerous books and resources that explain the benefits of teaching in units of study. The educator and author who has been most influential in our work with teachers is Katie Wood Ray, first in her book *About the Authors: Workshop with Our Youngest Authors* (with L. Cleaveland), and later in *Study Driven: A Framework for Planning Units of Study in the Writing Workshop.* In both of these books Katie makes a strong case for organizing your teaching into units, in intermediate as well as primary grades.

Katie writes, "By definition, mini lessons are short and focused. If they are not organized over time under an umbrella of a bigger topic of interest to people who write, then our whole-class teaching can have a very hit-and-miss feel to it" (Ray 2004, p. 106). We know numerous teachers who have this exact "hit-and-miss" feeling. They describe their teaching as disjointed, and wonder if they are heading in the right direction.

We, too, believe there are many advantages to organizing your teaching into units of study. Our unit projection process is designed to build on and extend the foundation that Katie and so many others have laid. Here are just some of the benefits:

- **It helps you think about and understand writing more deeply.** In a unit of study, you are going to study a stack of texts. In the process, you learn more about writing and the decisions that authors make.

- **A clearly named unit helps you prioritize and focus your teaching.** When you teach a unit, your students are working toward specific goals. These goals help you to organize your minilessons and conferences logically so they build toward your unit goals.

- **Units help you clarify expectations for students.** In any unit of study there are numerous skills and techniques students could learn. Some techniques and skills are essential, while others represent possible teaching points that might not be expectations for all students. When you are teaching a well-defined unit of study with clear goals, the goals determine the most essential learning points for students. And of course in order to have unit goals, you must be in a unit of study.

- **Units help students visualize the kinds of writers they can become.** In almost every unit students will be studying a stack of real-world, published writing that provides them with a vision for what they will create, or that will help them better understand what it means to be a writer. In genre-specific units these texts include examples of the genre. Many non-genre-specific units are organized by a common crafting element such as punctuation or structure. Even some process units use mentor texts, such as a stack of picture books for the unit Where Writers Get Ideas that includes information in the author's notes as to where the author got the idea for the book.

# Types of Units: Genre-Specific and Non-Genre-Specific

There are different ways to categorize the various types of units. We find it helpful to categorize units of study into two groups: *genre-specific* studies, which focus on a particular genre (e.g., Realistic Fiction), and *non-genre-specific* studies, in which students study a process of writing (e.g., Revision) or a product that is not related to a particular genre (e.g., Illustration). We also find it beneficial to pay attention to the ratio of genre-specific and non-genre-specific units being taught within a grade or a school. Many schools, districts, and states focus heavily on genre-specific studies. While these are important, we believe students also benefit from engaging in some non-genre-specific studies each year. The following sections explain in more detail what we mean by each type of unit.

## Genre-Specific Studies

Genre-specific studies are units of study in which "genre" is the organizing concept. The texts in a stack for a genre study are all in the same genre. The genre could be poetry, memoir, or informational how-to articles. If you can find a stack of texts within a certain genre, you can study it.

Katie Wood Ray explains, "Basically there are two main kinds of studies that make sense for writing workshop: studies that have something to do with the *process* of writing (and what it means to be a writer living through the process) or studies that have something to do with the *products* of writing . . . Genre study is really a marriage of the two because you study both the process of writing in the genre (and yes, the process is slightly different for different genres) and you study examples of the genre (the product) too." (2006, p. 83)

## TEACHING FOR TEST WRITING

Teachers are sometimes required to teach students how to create a type of writing that can't be found in the real world. This happens occasionally with writing that appears on state tests. For example, Matt was recently working in a state where students are required to write a three-paragraph essay as part of their state test. Of course, you can't find published three-paragraph essays in the real world. That doesn't mean you should study only fabricated three-paragraph essays. Students can learn to write essays well by studying longer published essays, and then learn to write a less complex (and less interesting) three-paragraph essay to prepare for a test. We always advocate studying real texts first, and then teaching students how to apply their writing knowledge to a less-sophisticated type of test writing.

Genre-specific studies tend to be the type of unit teachers are most familiar with. However, it's important to make sure that the genre exists in the real world outside of school. For example, stand-alone descriptive paragraphs are not a real-world genre. We can certainly teach students to write descriptively within a genre, but we want to make sure that we have real-world texts to study.

Genre-specific studies are important because they provide students with opportunities to read like writers as they study a stack of mentor texts while learning the process that a writer goes through to create a piece of writing in a particular genre. We believe students should gain experience with numerous genres throughout their years in elementary school because when they study mentor texts to learn how to produce something similar on their own, they are learning an important life-long writing skill. Throughout their lives they will encounter new genres (especially in our rapidly changing world), and they will need to learn how to write in them. A strong foundation in being able to study a genre in order to produce their own writing in that genre will serve them well. We want students not only to learn the specifics about writing in a variety of genres, but also to understand the *process* of studying a new genre and learning to write it.

### Non-Genre-Specific Studies

Non-genre-specific units are simply any units that are not genre studies. Within a non-genre-specific unit, you might study a *process* writers use (for example, Where Writers Get Ideas or How Authors Make Paragraphing Decisions, both units that Katie Wood Ray describes in her work), or you might study a *product* (such as illustrations or punctuation). You can examine the idea of finding topics, deciding when to start a new paragraph, and being thoughtful in your use of punctuation within a variety of genres.

The decision to teach non-genre-specific units is an important one because in these units *students choose* what genre to write in. Just like picking your own topic is a crucial factor in increasing motivation and energy for writing, so is choosing your genre (Glover 2009). When given the choice and support from a teacher, students will select the genre they have the most energy for. Therefore, we strongly encourage the use of some non-genre-specific units throughout the year. In particular, we encourage teachers at all grades

## EXAMPLES OF NON-GENRE-SPECIFIC STUDIES

### Primary Grades

Illustration Study

How Authors Use Punctuation in Interesting Ways

Reading Like a Writer

### Intermediate Grades

Using a Writer's Notebook

How to Have Better Peer Conferences

Generating Topics and Genres

to start the year with a non-genre-specific unit. At the beginning of the year we want to maximize energy for writing, because we know how unlikely it is that children will have a high level of motivation for writing in May if they're not motivated to write in September.

Sometimes teachers ask Matt, "Don't you have to teach about a genre before students can write in it?" Matt usually replies that he hasn't yet had a preschool student ask him, before writing her first book, "What genre should I write in?" Preschoolers will naturally write in a genre, or organize their book as a list or a story. They might write a fictional story about a princess or a book that tells the reader all about their family. Often their "books" include random things, aren't on topic, and are organized in a list rather than a story. We are not saying that preschoolers will write in a genre *well*, but they can't help but write in a genre (or at least have a genre-like organization). The same is true for older students, but of course we want them to be more intentional in their choice of genre. We want them to select genres for specific purposes and audiences, an important skill in being a writer. But if children are never in non-genre-specific units, they might never become skilled at making that choice.

It is easy to unintentionally turn a non-genre-specific study into a genre-specific study by including only one genre in your stack of mentor texts. All four of the units we've mentioned (Where Writers Get Ideas, Paragraphing Decisions, Punctuation, and Illustrations) could turn into de facto genre studies if the teacher includes only texts from a certain genre. If our stack for any of these units contains only fictional stories, then we are subtly communicating to students that this process or technique occurs only in that particular genre. If every book in our Where Writers Get Ideas unit is a story, then our unit is really Where Writers Get Ideas for Stories. In Appendix A we have included a list of possible units of study. You'll notice that some are genre specific, some are non-genre specific, and some could be either depending on the stack of texts chosen. Most of the other units listed could be genre specific or not, depending on what texts you include.

# Why *Project* Units of Study?

We believe that students will become better writers when we project a unit of study because we consider all of the possibilities. When we spend time projecting how a unit could unfold, we are ensuring that we are prepared to respond thoughtfully to the numerous opportunities to make decisions that comprise the world of teaching. When we project, we don't know for sure what techniques students will notice in the stack of texts for a unit, which concepts they will grasp quickly, or when they'll need more time. There are many unknowns, but by thinking ahead and projecting what *could* happen we are better prepared for whatever *does* happen. Projecting a unit provides the teacher with many advantages:

- **The projection process generates many possibilities for what could be taught in a unit of study.** We often hear from teachers that they want to teach a particular unit but don't know which techniques, processes, and skills to include. When teachers project and think ahead in a unit of study, they generate teaching possibilities based on a variety of sources. Projecting a unit of study generates a large pool of teaching possibilities for minilessons, conferences, and share/reflection times. During this process, the teacher considers more teaching possibilities than she will have time for, but by considering all of them, she is more able to make adjustments throughout the unit based on what arises day to day with students.

- **Teachers prioritize the important things to teach in a unit.** When teachers project a unit and consider the entire range of possible teaching points, they can then determine which points are more important than others to focus on during whole-group minilessons, conferences, and share/reflection times.

- **Teachers consider the sequence of minilesson topics.** When teachers project a sequence of teaching possibilities, they determine which topics could be taught together and which might be taught before others. Thinking about which teaching points are more important and when to teach them makes the instruction more connected and coherent for students, because it is logical and organized.

- **Decision making during writing conferences becomes more efficient and effective.** In an efficient conference, we need to decide quickly what teaching point will best meet a student's needs. We can do this effectively when we have already considered and prioritized. By thinking through a unit ahead of time, we can be more focused and effective during writing conferences.

## Balancing Teacher Direction with Student Inquiry

In any unit of study teachers will have to decide how inquiry-based the unit will be. The continuum spans units that are completely based on what students notice to units that are totally teacher directed, with day-by-day teaching determined before a unit starts. It's important to decide the level of inquiry and teacher direction you are comfortable with.

In an inquiry unit, the curriculum grows from what students notice when studying the stack of texts. As Katie Wood Ray states in *Study Driven*, "Framing instruction as study represents an essential stance to teaching and learning, an inquiry stance, characterized by repositioning curriculum as the outcome of instruction rather than the starting point. In this particular set of practices, the students' noticing and questioning around the gathered texts determines what will become important content in the study (the teacher doesn't determine this in advance), and depth rather than coverage is the driving force in the development of this content" (Ray 2006, p. 19). In an inquiry unit you can plan for inquiry by deepening your knowledge of the type of writing for the unit, and what an author does to create a text like the ones in the stack, but you will base much of your teaching on what students notice.

On the other end of the continuum is a teacher-directed unit, in which the teacher determines not what *could* be taught, but what *will* be taught. The teacher plans (rather than projects) what will be covered on each day of the unit. The teacher studies the stack of texts and directs students to notice certain things and try them in their writing.

Every unit probably has some elements of both inquiry and teacher direction. Most teachers are responsive to what students notice as well as determine some of what should be taught. But it is important to consider where on the continuum you want the unit to fall.

We certainly lean toward the inquiry end of this continuum and strive to make our own teaching as inquiry based as possible. We believe in the power of inquiry in all aspects of learning, including content areas other than writing. We also understand that for many teachers who are just starting to create units on their own, there is a comfort in predetermining much of what could be taught. If you are interested in learning more about inquiry in the writing workshop, check out *Study Driven* by Katie Wood Ray. Our goal in this book is to focus on the benefits and process of projecting a unit grounded in a stack of mentor texts, regardless of where the teacher envisions the unit landing on the inquiry continuum. We want to provide teachers with a vision for a process that allows for and expects student inquiry, yet isn't based solely on inquiry.

Our focus in projecting a unit is on *could* rather than *will*: The process for projecting is based on thinking about how a unit could unfold, while planning a unit means determining how the unit will unfold. The results of student inquiry into mentor texts, along with what happens with students each day in a unit, will impact how the unit of study grows and evolves.

# Building Opportunities for Incremental, Individualized Learning Throughout Unit Projection

Units of study help teachers organize their teaching in logical ways. We believe that students learn best when their learning is incremental, when each teaching interaction builds on the one that came before. The challenge is to teach children in nudges rather than pushes. Envisioning our teaching in this way is crucial to projecting units of study, whether we are thinking about whole-class nudges in minilessons or individual nudges during conferences.

We can think about the difference between nudges and pushes like this. Recently Matt's son Harrison was old enough to get his temporary driver's license. Matt quickly discovered that learning to drive is a study in nudging. During Harrison's first driving lesson, which occurred out in the country with no one around, Matt nudged his son's development by figuring out the smallest step Harrison could make without hurting anything. It was something like, "Take your foot off the brake, roll forward three feet, put your foot back on the brake." Then it was, "Drive forward at five miles an hour, then stop." Eventually it was, "Drive down this road at twenty-five miles an hour." It progressed like this for several days, with each lesson increasing the difficulty of the driving.

After several days, Harrison said, "OK Dad, I think I'm ready to start looking at the signs now." That sounds a bit terrifying to think that Harrison had been driving without looking at the signs, but without realizing it Harrison was perfectly describing the role of nudging. He was basically saying, "Up until now all I could do was try to steer the car without hitting anything. Now I can look at the signs. Soon I can look at the speedometer." He was learning in sensible increments. He was learning by being nudged. His early driving experience would have been very different if he had started out on I-75 in downtown Cincinnati, steering the car, looking at the signs, and monitoring his speed. That would have sent him over the edge. It would have been a push.

Nudging rather than pushing is important in teaching writing in units of study as well. One child's nudge is another child's push, so when we project teaching possibilities for a unit we are helping envision an array of nudges for the individual students in our classes. We need to be able to adjust our teaching for individual students. Our teaching decisions are based on what we know about the individual child sitting in front of us as well as what we know about writing. For example, in a unit of study on poetry, our focus for one student might be on trying to use line breaks so her poem looks like a poem; for the next child it might be using similes as a way of describing something. We might teach the next child how to use a narrative structure in her poem. The unit goals are the same, but the individual nudges change from student to student.

Projecting a unit of study helps us design teaching that moves children forward with nudges, not pushes. When figuring out what represents a nudge, we have to first look at what the child is doing independently, and then decide what one small step will help her move forward. When we organize our teaching into units of study, and project how the unit could unfold, we create an array of possible nudges that we can use in any given minilesson or writing conference. Watching what a class or student is doing and selecting a nudge is a decision that only a thoughtful teacher can make. The process for projecting a unit of study described in the rest of this book will help your nudges become more logical, thoughtful, and beneficial for your students. In the next chapter, we give you an outline of the process that can help you begin this important work.

# Projecting a Unit of Study

## A Process Overview

Whether you are preparing for a trip or projecting a unit, it helps to know where you are going before you start. In this chapter we'll give a brief overview of the entire process for projecting a unit. The remaining chapters will examine each step in greater depth.

Anyone who knows Matt knows that he's not a naturally organized person. When Matt was a principal, his office was not a model of efficiency, and if it hadn't been for an amazingly kind, patient, and understanding secretary, he might have been trapped under an avalanche of papers and books. When Matt started consulting and doing workshops, his organizational deficiencies followed him. At the end of a workshop he would quickly pack his computer and presentation equipment to make it to a plane on time, and invariably leave something behind. A DVD in Houston, a laptop power cord in Boston, a projector connection cable in Cleveland.

Pretty soon Matt grew tired of calling districts the day after his visit and asking them to mail the DVD that he left in the DVD player. He decided that he needed a process for packing up at the end of each day, and that he needed to do it the same way each time. Now, he goes through specific steps in the same order each time he packs up—first the adaptors go into the right front pocket of the computer bag, next the power cord goes into the main compartment, followed by the DVDs in the front right pocket, then the external hard drive in the front left inside pocket, and so on. Being this organized is counter to Matt's nature but he sticks to his process out of necessity. Having a process and using it consistently has worked.

# The Importance of Having a Process

Having a process is important for anything you do repeatedly. Using a process has several advantages:

- Your actions become more habitual and easy to repeat. By doing the same things over and over each time, your actions become routine.

- Your actions are more logical. Processes that work are processes that make sense.

- You can transfer your process to new situations.

- Your process becomes a habit of mind, more a way of thinking than a series of steps. You become less aware of the process as it becomes ingrained in your thinking.

Many of the teachers we work with are looking for just such a process to help them create their own units. Creating units certainly requires deeper thinking than simply remembering what to pack up at the end of the day. However, whether the process requires deep thinking or not, the key is to have a system that you can replicate and that will make your work more efficient.

There are many different ways to project a unit of study, but we have found the process we'll describe to be helpful and efficient as we design responsive units in writing workshop. Our hope is that using this process will make projecting units of study more logical, more repeatable, and just plain easier. We also hope to encourage those who are new to designing their own units to give it a try.

# Projecting a Unit of Study: The Steps of the Process

Following this outline of the process is a brief explanation of each step and a reference to the chapter that covers it in detail.

1. Decide on and name the unit of study.

2. Gather and study a stack of mentor texts, pulling out teaching possibilities as you read.

**3.** Determine primary and secondary goals.

**4.** Project possible minilesson topics.

**5.** Anticipate and prepare for issues.

**6.** Respond during the unit and reflect when the unit is completed.

## 1. Decide on and Name the Unit of Study

To project a unit you must first decide what units to teach throughout the year and name them carefully. You must take into account curriculum and standards to choose units to meet your school's requirements. You must consider what you know about your students in order to select units that will meet their needs and boost their energy for writing. You will also consider your own writing passions.

It is helpful to begin the year with a list of units you will definitely teach (critical units) and a longer list of units you *might* teach (possible units). You'll have a basic plan for your year of teaching, but you'll know that you will make changes as the year unfolds, based on the needs of your students.

After deciding on the unit you will project and teach first, you must thoughtfully name it. Choosing a name that reflects specifically what you hope to teach will clarify and solidify your aim, and will also be helpful as you determine unit goals. (See Chapter 4 for more detail.)

## 2. Gather and Study a Stack of Mentor Texts, Pulling Out Teaching Possibilities as You Read

For most units, the projecting process starts with gathering a stack of mentor texts that are good examples of the writing students will create, and reading them like a teacher of writers. As you read, use all that you know about teaching writing and all that you know about your students to start making a list of all of the teaching possibilities the texts offer. When you notice something that an author does in a text, write it on the list. During this phase write down *everything* that you think you might teach and that students might notice when they are immersed in the texts during the unit. At first, you just want to look at *possibilities*. You'll focus your list later in the process.

When you have finished studying these texts and made a long list of teaching possibilities, you'll have a much clearer sense of the unit's content. At this point you can expand your knowledge by reading what literacy experts say. Numerous resources provide background knowledge about various units of study. It also can be invaluable to go through this process with a group of colleagues. Different teachers will notice different teaching possibilities, broadening the group's sense of what could be taught.

It's also important to note that we are describing the process *teachers* go through in studying mentor texts before projecting a unit. We study the texts again with *students* during the immersion phase as the unit begins. Students will notice some of the same things we did as well as items we missed when studying on our own. Studying texts with students often requires us to make adjustments to our unit projection based on what they noticed. (See Chapter 5 for more detail.)

### 3. Determine Primary and Secondary Goals

After studying your stack of mentor texts and listing teaching possibilities, it is important to consider the unit's broader goals—both primary and secondary. Primary goals describe the one to three broad, overarching objectives for this unit. They are the really big ideas and skills you want students to be able to know and do at the end of this unit that they can't do now. They are what most of your minilessons and student conferences will build toward.

After determining primary goals, you'll set four to eight secondary goals. These goals are more specific than the primary goals, and often describe what a chunk of lessons will focus on. Secondary goals focus on a variety of different elements of being a writer and writing well. Most units will have goals related to the qualities of good writing and the writing process as well as goals for revision and editing. (See Chapter 6 for more detail.)

### 4. Project Possible Minilesson Topics

Once you've set primary and secondary goals, you'll list a possible sequence of minilesson topics. Use the list of teaching possibilities you wrote down as you studied your stack of texts. You'll have many more teaching possibilities than available teaching days. As you look at this list, do three things:

- Determine which topics are the most important to teach, and therefore deserve to be taught during minilessons. The other items don't go on the projected sequence of lessons, but they aren't forgotten either. At any point they might be needed for a minilesson or conference.

- Determine which things would make sense to be taught together and group them into chunks.

- Determine the projected sequence of lesson topics.

Again, this is only a projection, and will likely not be exactly how the lessons unfold once the unit begins. (See Chapter 7 for more detail.)

## 5. Anticipate and Prepare for Issues

As you consider possible minilessons, some topics you will be pretty certain you'll need to teach. Others you won't be sure about. There will also be some topics with which only a few students are apt to need help. It is important to prepare to meet the needs of all students, individually or in small-group conferences. The minilesson topics provide a possible course for whole-class teaching, but you also need to plan for students who need additional support as well as those who might benefit from enrichment.

You will want to record your thinking as you consider the needs of individuals within your class and the unknown aspect of how your teaching will progress with the whole class. So that they aren't forgotten, use the Anticipated Issues section of the template (see Appendix B) to record teaching possibilities that reflect the needs

### INSIGHTS FROM A PRINCIPAL

In our teachers' first session (using the unit projection process), we spent almost two hours planning goals and brainstorming possible teaching points. One year in, our entire school has begun to implement this process of projecting units. Essential and secondary goals drive what we teach and assess. Teachers use stacks of books to mine for teaching points and skills to teach; they refer to these in their minilessons and individual conferences. Most powerfully, it has brought consistency in collaboratively deciding on what is most essential to assess in student writing. It also provides teachers flexibility in how it is taught. Instead of having teaching points driving our units, we now have common goals, and our day-to-day teaching is determined on what is best for the individual students in individual classrooms.

It now takes a team of nine teachers forty-five minutes to plan out the essential and secondary goals for a unit and briefly brainstorm some ideas for teaching points, while our literacy coach collates our collective knowledge into a common unit template. In one year, our entire kindergarten writing curriculum has undergone this process. As we analyze our student's writing, we are beginning to see more consistency and improvement across the grade levels, and the rich conversations that result among teachers help us to make improvements in future units.

—*Ben Hart, Associate Principal, Hong Kong*

of small groups of students along with minilesson topics you're not sure you'll need. This section functions as a parking lot for potential issues, reminders, and possible-small group conferences. (See Chapter 7 for more detail.)

### 6. Respond During the Unit and Reflect When the Unit Is Completed

As you teach the unit, you will make decisions that will alter the path of your teaching. You may decide to add a minilesson topic or take one out. You might decide to spend more or less time on a topic. You might decide to teach a lesson earlier or later than you had anticipated. Record these changes on the projection template so these decisions can inform the projection of your unit next year.

Once you have finished teaching the unit, it is crucial that you and your colleagues spend some time reflecting on the unit. What went well? What changes were made during the unit? What needs to be tweaked for next year? How will discussions, questions, and "noticings" that arose in this unit affect your next unit? Spending even a few minutes writing down your reflections will make the next unit projection process even more informed. (See Chapter 8 for more detail.)

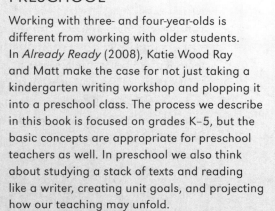

## A WORD ABOUT PRESCHOOL

Working with three- and four-year-olds is different from working with older students. In *Already Ready* (2008), Katie Wood Ray and Matt make the case for not just taking a kindergarten writing workshop and plopping it into a preschool class. The process we describe in this book is focused on grades K–5, but the basic concepts are appropriate for preschool teachers as well. In preschool we also think about studying a stack of texts and reading like a writer, creating unit goals, and projecting how our teaching may unfold.

In *Already Ready,* Katie and Matt talk about writing instruction with young children, including the concept of focus ideas rather than units of study. A focus idea is simply an organizing focus for writing-focused read-alouds that will occur periodically over several weeks. Thinking ahead about what your writing goals are and how the books and experiences you select will help your students reach these goals will make your teaching more intentional and effective.

## Working with the Projection Template

Throughout this book we will refer to a projection template that many teachers have found to be helpful. At first we were surprised that teachers asked us for a copy of our projection template since it is basically headings and blank space, but as teachers ourselves, we know that it is often easier to start with something rather than staring at a blank piece of paper. We've included a full-size template in Appendix B; a condensed version is shown in Figure 3.1. You can also download a projection template from www.heinemann.com/products/E04192.aspx. We recommend keeping a copy of the template in your computer as you project a unit. Working in an electronic document makes it much easier to rearrange, insert, or delete lessons.

As you can see, the projection template has sections for each part of the process we just described. It's important to note that the numbers are meant to suggest only a *rough* idea of the number of goals or minilessons in a unit; you might have more or fewer goals, and the number of minilesson topics will depend on how long your unit is.

It is also important to realize that the projection template continues to evolve. As our thinking changes we add sections, change the wording, and modify the layout. It's likely that by the time this book comes out our projection template will look different than it appears here. That's why having it available online is helpful. For one thing, we'll update the online template as we make changes. But more importantly,

**Figure 3.1** Projection Template

Unit of Study: _____

_____ Genre Specific   _____ Non-Genre Specific   _____ # of Weeks

**Primary Goals:**
1.
2.
3.

**Secondary Goals:** Writing Quality, Writing Habits, Revision, Community of Writers, Editing/Conventions
1.
2.
3.
4.
5.
6.

**Anticipated Issues:**
1.
2.

**Projection of Possible Mini Lesson Topics:**
1.
2.
3.

4.
5.
6.
7.
8.
9.
10.
11.
12.
13.
14.
15.
16.
17.
18.
19.
20.

**Other Teaching Possibilities:**
1.

**Resources/Materials/Books:** Mentor texts, professional resources, etc.

**Reflections:**

having it online allows you to modify the form and create one that best meets your individual needs. Just as one unit can't fit the needs of every class, one projection template can't anticipate and meet the needs of every teacher.

The unit projection process is equally valuable for projecting both a unit you haven't taught before and a unit that you know well. We always project units, even units we know like the back of our hand, because every year our students change. Even if you've taught a unit many times, you need to think it through with each year's students in mind and build on what you've learned about the type of writing by studying it with previous classes. This process helps your teaching become more personalized and therefore more effective.

Our experience is that this process for projecting a unit of study is both manageable and beneficial. We find that it gives teachers a path that leads to well-thought-out units that improve the quality of teaching and learning. Of course, as with any process, there is more to think about than just what the individual steps are. Whether the process is packing a bag at the end of a workshop or projecting a unit of study, there is solid reason for each step. The subsequent chapters will provide important rationales and explanations for each step in the process.

# What Should I Teach?

## Choosing Units of Study

The working title of this book at one time was *What Should I Teach?* because that is the question we hear most frequently from teachers. More specifically, teachers always ask us:

- Which units should I teach during a year?
- How do I decide which minilesson to teach next?
- How do I decide what to teach in a conference?

We love to hear these questions because they show that a teacher is thinking critically about her students and making decisions based on their needs. We believe that teachers should decide which writing workshop units will engage their students, what minilesson makes sense on any given day, and what to teach in a conference. Teachers certainly need to teach from standards and curriculum; we're not advocating they just teach whatever strikes their fancy. But ultimately, teachers can best decide what units and lessons will meet state and district goals as well as the needs of their students.

## Critical and Possible Units

In the many schools we work in, the district expects that teachers will include several common units across a grade level as well as units they select themselves. We often refer to them as *critical* and *possible* units. There are usually four or five critical units that all students in a grade level will experience. These are decided on at the school or district level to ensure common experiences across a grade. There is also a more flexible list of possible units that a teacher will choose from according to the needs and interests of her students. A teacher may even decide to do a unit at some point in the year that isn't on the list.

In many schools, the primary grades list of critical units includes a unit to launch writer's workshop, some type of story writing unit, some type of nonfiction unit, and a poetry unit. There is also usually a non-genre-specific unit such as Using Punctuation in Interesting Ways or Text Structure. Another unit might be Author Study. Intermediate grades tend to use more genre-specific units. Common topics are Launching Writer's Workshop or Launching the Use of a Writer's Notebook. In each intermediate grade there would also be various units on narrative, informational, and opinion writing. Poetry could also certainly be a critical unit.

Table 4.1 shows just one example of how a school might determine critical and possible units. These are not intended as suggested units, but rather as an example of one way of organizing units that supports teacher choice and decision making. You will, of course, make your own decisions regarding units based on your students, district expectations, and other factors influencing you. See Appendix C or go to www.heinemann.com/products/E04192.aspx for a blank template to use for keeping track of your own critical and possible units.

Having a balance of critical and possible units takes into account both the need to meet common expectations and the importance of teacher choice. It also allows schools to consider the placement of units from year to year to avoid teaching some units repeatedly and others not at all.

 We realize that in some situations, teachers will not have the freedom to determine which units they will teach or what will be taught within a unit. In some schools, curricular calendars are predetermined. Our concern with calendars that prescribe what is to be taught every day of the year is that they limit a teacher's ability to answer the question "Why are you in this unit at this point in the year?" in a way that reflects the ability to respond to the needs of her particular class. If the answer is only that it's next on the calendar, then the teacher isn't being encouraged to consider the needs and interests of her students in addition to district requirements when determining units.

If you work in a school like this, don't worry. Our hope is that even in these situations there are opportunities for teachers to make choices. We recognize that in many schools, teachers are working within a less flexible structure, but the good news is that even in more restrictive contexts, teachers can make meaningful decisions to ensure that their teaching matches their students' needs.

For example, Matt was recently working in a first grade in a district that had decided that the entire first quarter of the year would be devoted to a unit on personal

**Figure 4.1:** Sample Critical and Possible Units

| Kindergarten | |
|---|---|
| **Critical Units** | **Possible Units** |
| Launching Writer's Workshop | Author Study |
| Illustration Study | Where Writers Get Ideas |
| Stories from My Life | Reading Like a Writer |
| Nonfiction All-About Books | How-To Books |
| | Literary Nonfiction |
| | Craft Study |
| | Poetry |
| | Any teacher-created unit |

| Fourth Grade | |
|---|---|
| **Critical Units** | **Possible Units** |
| Using a Writer's Notebook | Memoir |
| Writing Reviews | How-To Articles |
| Short Stories of Realistic Fiction | Mysteries |
| Feature Articles | Commentary |
| Poetry | Travel Articles |
| | Advice Writing |
| | Where Writers Get Ideas/What Types of Things Do Writers Make?/Finding Writing Projects |
| | Slice of Life |
| | Biographical Sketches/Profiles |
| | Any teacher-created unit |

narrative writing. After discussing their concerns about this, as well as the need for students to have the opportunity to choose their own genre, the teachers thought that they might be able to tweak the schedule while still following the district curriculum map. They decided to spend the first four weeks of the quarter in an illustration study and the last five weeks in the required personal narrative study. Not only would five weeks be sufficient to cover the district's required personal narrative material, but students' personal narrative writing would be much stronger as a result of the increase in compositional thinking and energy that the illustration study would produce. Since they were meeting district goals and requirements and had a strong rationale for their proposal, their principal supported this adaptation of district requirements.

Later in this chapter we'll explore how to decide which units to teach, but first let's look at several sources that influence the choices we make.

# The Big Picture: What Influences Unit Choice?

There are many sources to consider when deciding which units of study to pursue with your students.

### Standards and Curriculum

Standards help ensure that students across a state or district are taught the same content and work toward common goals. Most states have grade-level indicators for writing and test student writing proficiency at some point during the elementary years. These tests are based on the state standards, so state departments of education have determined some of what should be taught.

Most states have adopted the Common Core State Standards (CCSS), which are designed to specify broad goals. They give you room to project units of your choosing, while meeting the standards at the same time. For example, one of the Common Core standards requires students to produce narrative writing and describes how the complexity of narrative writing should grow from year to year. However, the Common Core doesn't require a certain genre to be taught. To meet the narrative writing standard, students could study realistic fiction, fiction, memoir, or other genres that have the traits of that standard.

The Common Core State Standards, like any standards, are most useful when teachers are able to make decisions for themselves about how to meet them. Keep in mind that the standards themselves are not designed to dictate specific unit choice.

## THINKING BEYOND STATE WRITING STANDARDS

Another consideration when thinking about standards is that sometimes state standards underestimate what children can do. For example, many state standards in early childhood (PreK–2) are so focused on the conventions of writing (spelling, punctuation, etc.) that they underestimate the depth of composition that young children are capable of achieving. Teachers can ensure that the units they choose include practice with developing skills and techniques beyond writing conventions. For example, deciding how to have your pictures and text work together is a big skill for young children yet it often isn't accounted for in standards and curriculum documents. Often early writing is seen only as an entry point into reading rather than supporting writing for writing's sake (Ray and Glover 2008). While there is certainly a strong connection between early writing and reading, educators should also support children's ability to make decisions that impact how a piece of writing is composed.

### District Curricula

District curriculum guides are usually based on state standards, but also provide more specifics about what material teachers are expected to cover. By their very nature, district curricula provide goals and benchmarks that students should work toward. District curricula may provide guidelines for critical units for each grade level to ensure all children across a district are taught the same material. When choosing units of study for your class, it's important to look at both state standards and district curricula so you're sure to choose units that you can tie to the goals they present. While more specific than Common Core or other state standards, district

## CHOOSING UNITS THAT RELATE TO STANDARDS

### First-Grade Language Arts Standard from the Common Core

**Writing Standard 1.1:** Write informative/explanatory texts in which they name a topic, supply some facts about the topic, and provide some sense of closure.

Paul, a first-grade teacher, compared the units he was planning on teaching one year with the Common Core standards. One unit, called Information All-About Books, seemed to match this standard well. Using this standard as a baseline, students learned about informative/explanatory writing by making books that teach the reader all about various topics. In this unit, students easily met this standard. Paul projected the unit to elaborate on this standard as well as to hit several of the speaking and listening standards.

### Fourth-Grade Language Arts Standard from the Common Core

**Writing Standard 4.3:** Write narratives to develop real or imagined experiences or events using effective technique, descriptive details, and clear event sequences.

After starting her year with several non-genre-specific units, Chloe, a fourth-grade teacher, decided to move into a genre-specific unit with her students. Knowing that the standards required her to do some type of narrative writing, she decided on the unit True Stories from My Life. By structuring minilessons that helped her students understand sequence and how to show movement through time, she was able to provide scaffolds for students to create their own personal narratives that included descriptive details and clear event sequences.

curricula are not likely to provide the specificity needed for projecting which mini-lessons to include in a unit, nor will they help you meet the individual needs of students in your classes. However, they are an important beginning to deciding on your units of study.

Our responsibility as teachers is to take state standards and district curricula, consider our current students, and translate these factors into learning experiences that provide meaningful nudges forward on a daily basis. States and districts can determine the big curriculum objectives for a year, but only a skilled teacher can determine what should be taught in individual classes and to individual students each day. States and districts can't make day-to-day decisions for teachers.

## Day-by-Day Writing Programs and Unit Resources

Many districts and schools have chosen to follow particular writing programs. In some cases the developer of the program intended that the program be followed day by day. Other unit resources were actually designed for teachers to reinterpret and make their own, but have been misinterpreted and misused by districts, and implemented in much the same way as a writing program. Regardless of whether a program is intended to be followed as a script or not, there are some things to consider regarding programs and curricular guides.

A writing program can help you keep goals in mind as you choose and project units of study. Some programs even help you predict specific teaching points. We believe, however, that packaged programs should not determine your day-by-day decisions. For example, as you begin a unit on feature articles you will probably teach your students how to organize their articles into sections. A writing program would likely contain some lessons on how to do this. But the program wouldn't know if your students grasped this concept quickly and were ready to move on, or if they struggled to organize their articles and needed additional support. Programs can help you see the broad strokes of what could be included in a unit, but they can't help you make decisions that grow from watching and working with your students. As the classroom teacher, *you* are best positioned to make decisions about what mini-lesson would be most beneficial on any particular day in a unit of study.

Unit resources that are designed as planning resources rather than scripts can be helpful, so long as you examine these units *after* you've projected your own unit. In fact, the best unit resources we've seen are designed to be outgrown and aim to provide a teacher with one possible vision of how a unit could be followed. It can be very helpful to look at another unit, whether a published unit or one created by a colleague. Reviewing someone else's unit might generate teaching goals or teaching possibilities that you hadn't considered. For example, a group of teachers planning a unit on the photo essay might look at someone else's plan, see a series of lessons on how to write captions succinctly, and then decide to include that skill in their unit. You don't have to follow someone else's unit exactly, but it can inform the unit you create.

It's also important to realize that some programs and resources are better than others. These are some of the questions you might ask as you evaluate a program:

- Is the program grounded in real-world mentor texts?
- Are children engaged in thinking about and exploring these texts?
- Are children noticing similarities across texts and discussing the decisions the authors made?
- Are students making the same type of text that they are studying? (For example, if they're studying picture books, are they making picture books?)
- Does the program allow for student choice of topic?
- Do some units allow students to choose their genre?
- Does the program have an appropriate balance in focus between composition and conventions?
- Does the program help students understand the qualities of good writing?

Teachers may not always be able to give input regarding whether a program or resource is to be used, but understanding the qualities of good writing instruction can help teachers influence decisions about what is purchased, and hopefully how it is used.

## Professional Books

When projecting a unit of study, teachers can use professional books focused on that particular unit as a way of understanding more about the unit's possible goals. If we're preparing to project a unit of study on memoir, for example, we might first look at state standards and district curricula to see if there are any standards or objectives for writing memoir. We would consider whether there are standards related to memoir even if they don't mention it specifically. We could also look at Katherine Bomer's book *Writing a Life*, a wonderful book focused solely on memoir. We could look at what Katie Wood Ray says about teaching memoir and where to find memoir stacks in *Study Driven*. We could take a look at Lucy Calkins unit of study book, *Memoir: The Art of Writing Well*. All of these resources would help us think more deeply about writing memoir.

Professional books offer us a wide range of ideas, research, and theory about our teaching and the units we wish to project. They allow us to participate in a larger conversation about students that extends far beyond our classrooms. This improves our teaching and the experiences of our students. It also helps us clarify what works for our teaching styles and the classrooms we have at the moment.

One year at our school we had reading experts Kathy Collins and Ellin Keene work with our teachers. Teachers would sometimes say, "Kathy said this, but Ellin said something different. What should we do?" Even though this was usually a nuanced reading issue (since Kathy and Ellin agree on so much), the question was sometimes accompanied by a sense of frustration on the part of the teacher. Instead of frustration, we embraced this as an opportunity to think. "What do *you* think about what they said? What makes sense to you, and why?" When teachers grapple with such questions they come to a deeper understanding of the hows and whys of teaching.

When looking at professional books' varied angles, we want to look at consistencies between what authors say, since that will provide a strong foundation for the key concepts in the unit. But we'd also expect (and want) there to be differences in how these authors and resources approach, for example, a unit on memoir. We want to consider divergent viewpoints and come to our own conclusions on how this unit will unfold for our particular class.

### Finding a Balance

Fortunately for teachers, we have many resources at our fingertips when making decisions about what units to teach and what to teach within each unit. To prepare units of study that fit the needs of our students, we need to know how to study a stack of mentor texts, pull out the key skills and techniques that students can learn from those texts, and relate those skills and techniques to a unit's goals (as we'll talk about in Chapter 5). When we have a stack of texts to show us (and our students) what good writing looks like, and when we have colleagues who can help us name what the authors do well, we are well on the way to projecting a responsive unit. We encourage you to trust your own ability to inquire and to study texts—you can learn what writers do and then share what you learn with your students.

We're not saying that teachers should be making up curricula or setting their own standards. There are common understandings about the qualities of good writing and how to support students in using a process to accomplish writing goals. There need to be shared beliefs about what it means to be a proficient writer at a particular grade level. And there are established characteristics of genres that lead to key skills and techniques to be learned when writing in a genre. You should have

# DIFFERENT TEACHERS, DIFFERENT INTERPRETATIONS

One year Mary Alice and her first-grade colleagues Kaelin and Asha were planning on teaching the same units throughout the year. They started with Genre Overview and then went into Illustration Study. From there they planned to go into a unit on writing, True Stories from Your Life. However, Mary Alice noticed that her students were still developing their stamina and energy for writing, and she felt that they needed an additional non-genre-specific unit that would continue to allow them to choose the genre they had the most energy for. So, Mary Alice decided to flip units and go into one called Reading Like a Writer. Meanwhile, Kaelin and Asha observed that their students had lots (and lots and lots) of energy for writing, and were composing long, rambling books. They wanted to help them focus their writing and develop their ability to organize it, so they stuck with their original plan to move into True Stories from Your Life. By observing their students and noticing what children were doing from day to day, each teacher could determine which unit would work best for his or her class.

The same type of decision making can occur within a unit. Mary Alice and Asha both started the year with a genre overview, a study in which students develop their skill in selecting genres and becoming articulate about their choice of genre. They both planned several minilessons early in the unit that would help students understand the difference between story books and list books, and realize that authors decide what type of book they are going to make before they start. Asha discovered that after three minilessons her students grasped this concept. During conferences her students were able to tell her what type of book they were making. So, she decided to move ahead and start to look at specific genres. Meanwhile, Mary Alice noticed that her students needed more time understanding story books and list books and decided to spend two additional minilessons reading books on the same topic in different genres (such as Marla Frazee's *Roller Coaster* and an informational book on roller coasters, or the story *Long Shot* by basketball player Chris Paul and an informational book about Chris Paul). After the two additional days she reassessed whether she needed to linger on this concept or move on (they were ready to move on).

In both of these situations the teachers are teaching within the context of their state and district standards. And, their decisions are grounded in what they know about teaching writing. But they are the ones making informed, thoughtful decisions about which units and which lessons to teach based on what they observe students doing within their classrooms.

a firm understanding about the teaching of writing, and there are resources to help you strengthen your knowledge base (see Appendix D). But only you can decide what will best move your class and individual students forward unit by unit and day by day.

# Making Decisions: Choosing Which Units You'll Teach Across the Year

Once you know what you are required to teach, you can decide what units to teach across the year. We think this long-range planning is important—if you have an idea of which units you're going to teach, you can be looking out for relevant mentor texts (keeping in mind, however, that the sequence or actual units could change). Of course, we absolutely advocate for teachers to have the ability to insert (or swap) a unit midway through the year based on what's going on in their room. Here are some answers to frequently asked questions that may help you in making your own decisions.

## What Types of Units Should Be Taught?

It is important to consider the balance of different types of units across a year. Use these guiding principles to help determine the types of units to include.

1.  **Include both genre-specific and non-genre-specific units.** Students should have opportunities to choose their genres as well as their topics. (For more on the difference between genre-specific and non-genre-specific units, see Chapter 2.) While genre-based studies occur more frequently as students get older, there is still a need for non-genre-specific units in the intermediate grades. When building a plan for units, consider where genre-specific and non-genre-specific units will occur in each grade.

2.  **Balance units from various modes of writing.** It is likely students will study some type of narrative writing each year (and possibly more than one) as well as a form of informational/explanatory writing. Students will also study various units involving opinion or persuasive writing. Teachers and administrators could look at the units in their grade, or across the grades, for a balance in the units that use these modes of writing.

3.  **Consider a balance of product studies and process studies.** In this case, balance doesn't mean equal, but that both types of studies are incorporated. We see many classrooms where students never encounter

a process study. In both primary and intermediate grades we think it's important to include units based on the study of some aspect of the process of writing. As Katie Wood Ray wrote, "We want children to leave our studies able to envision new possibilities for their writing—and we mean writing as a verb and a noun. Studies of the various aspects of the process of writing help children go about their writing work (writing as verb) in new ways, and studies of the products of writing (writing as a noun) help children realize new possibilities in the actual texts they compose" (Ray 2004, p. 103).

### What Units Make Sense for My Grade Level?

There are numerous possible units that could be taught at any particular grade level, more than could ever be taught in a given year. But when we look at possible units for K–2 or grades 3–6 (see Appendix A), we can see that some units might be better for one grade in that grouping than another. We don't rule out any units, but some may work better for the higher grades, based on the developmental needs of students. Here are two examples:

- In kindergarten, we wouldn't typically jump to How Authors Use Punctuation in Interesting Ways (a unit Katie Wood Ray describes in *About the Authors*). We know kindergarten teachers who have taught such a unit successfully late in the year, but it might be better to wait until first or second grade, when students tend to write more sentences on a page and have more of a need for punctuation.

- In grades 3–6 students could study essays, but we usually stay away from this genre in third or fourth grade. It's not that third and fourth graders can't write essays, but we tend to wait until fifth or sixth grade when it is easier to find age-appropriate published essays to use as mentor texts for this challenging type of writing.

### How Do I Plan the Sequence of Units?

Just as we want teachers to have some choice about which units to teach, we feel it also makes sense for teachers to have some flexibility with regard to the sequence of units. We want teachers to make thoughtful decisions based on the needs of their students while considering their growth as writers from unit to unit.

For example, one year Mary Alice was planning on engaging students in a punctuation study in January and a poetry unit in May. However, toward the end of the punctuation unit she decided to change the order. Her students had been thinking so much about the ways punctuation impacts how their writing sounds that she decided it made sense to capitalize on this by going right from punctuation into poetry, since much of the focus in poetry is how it sounds to the reader. Mary Alice was able to try this switch and see how well it worked. As a thoughtful teacher, she could examine the change and decide whether to keep these units together or apart the following year. If she had been confined to an overly rigid, lock-step calendar, she would have missed the opportunity to engage in the type of research and reflection that fosters teacher growth.

Some content areas, like math, require that some skills be taught before others. Writing is different—although some skills do come before others, there are few prerequisites in terms of sequencing units of study. As Katie Wood Ray says in *Study Driven*, "There is no magical right answer to what students should be studying at different grade levels at different times of the year. The design of the writing workshop itself, a place where students work over time to complete personally meaningful writing projects, gives rise to the most important curriculum as students develop the understandings and strategies of writers at work" (2006, p. 92).

A unit on realistic fiction doesn't have to come before literary nonfiction. Poetry doesn't have to come at the end of the year. While writing skills will build from unit to unit, one type of writing isn't more important than another. As Katie Wood Ray says, "Because craft crosses genre, as long as students are studying well-written texts it doesn't matter what genre they are in, they will see the same kinds of crafting elements." For example, students will learn how to use dialogue skillfully in any unit where they are writing a story, regardless of whether it's realistic fiction or fantasy. In any genre-specific unit, much of what is learned is representative of high-quality writing in general.

That said, there are some considerations in terms of timing:

- **Begin with a non-genre-specific unit.** When students choose their genre, their energy for writing increases. Recently Matt was teaching a class of fourth graders how to consider multiple genres from a single topic. The range of genres students eventually chose included personal essay, feature article, how-to article, personal narrative, mystery, fantasy, and fiction. They all chose the genre that motivated and interested them the most.

- **Teach more challenging units later in the year.** In fourth grade we might study review writing early in the year because it's a more concise, clear type of writing and save fantasy writing for later in the year when students' experience as writers will help them tackle this more challenging genre.

- **Begin with units that students can utilize throughout the year.** In the primary grades there are advantages to having an illustration study early in the year so that students can utilize the illustration techniques they learn as they compose illustrations in their books throughout the year. Or, in the intermediate grades, it would make sense to teach the unit Using a Writer's Notebook early in the year so students understand right from the start how to use a notebook as a tool in their writing.

- **Consider coordinating reading and writing instruction.** If you knew that your class was going to be in the study How to Get Information from a Nonfiction Text in reading, you could schedule your unit on Feature Articles to start a week after students begin reading feature articles in reading workshop. Or, a character study unit in a primary reading workshop might coordinate well with a realistic fiction writing unit since students will need to develop characters for the stories they write. The key here is to remember that every reading unit may not have a writing unit counterpart, so you should coordinate these only when it makes sense.

### How Often Should Units Be Repeated from Grade to Grade?

Because there are so many possible units for students to experience and benefit from, there are advantages to studying a variety of units across the grades. Coordinating units across grades takes some planning and communication. For example, think about a school where students study memoir six years in a row. By the time a child is in seventh grade in this school, she might be a bit "memoired" out. If teachers aren't planning across grades, they might not even realize that students are studying the same units year after year. The bigger problem is that the child has missed out on other units that would have stretched her thinking and fostered her growth as a writer. Having a variety of different units across the years helps expand writing skills that students can continue to use as they become more experienced writers.

However, there certainly are units that will spiral from year to year throughout the elementary grades. Students can think very differently about units at different ages as they gain more experience as writers. Therefore, there are advantages to revisiting units throughout the primary or intermediate grades. For example, you might study feature articles in third grade and again in fifth grade. The expectation is that a fifth grader's feature article will be more sophisticated than a third grader's. A fifth grader's feature articles would contain more information about their topic and be more engaging to read. They might publish them on the computer, which would allow for decisions about layout. And they would be able to bring two additional years of crafting skills and conventions knowledge to their work.

Sometimes there may be an advantage to studying the same unit in back-to-back years. Let's think again about feature articles. It might make sense to study them in fourth grade and again the following year. Students would be introduced to them in fourth grade and write them for the first time. Then the fifth-grade unit could go deeper, or include research, since students would already have a good understanding of feature articles from the previous year. Both of these scenarios describe advantages of revisiting units without suggesting that students study feature articles every single year.

## Flexibility Is Key

There are advantages to having a flexible plan for the year. If you have a good idea of what units you will probably teach, you can be on the lookout for mentor texts. You are much more likely to clip a great commentary from the newspaper or remember the title of a literary nonfiction picture book you found in the bookstore if you know you are going to teach that unit in the upcoming year.

Having a plan for the year gives you a direction and a framework. And, if you build flexibility and choice into the plan, you can design learning experiences that best meet your students' needs. Having a plan also keeps your teaching moving. It is easy to get stuck in one type of writing for too long. Having a plan helps you move forward so students don't lose energy, but also ensures that you avoid "hit-and-run" teaching by giving enough time to a unit for in-depth learning to take place.

We have decided not to include a sample calendar of units. We think it is much more beneficial for teachers and administrators to consider the factors listed above and build their own calendars. We believe that unit calendars are starting rather than ending points. Instead of including sample calendars, we have included lists of possible units of study for both primary and intermediate grades (see Appendix A). The hope is that these lists open up possibilities for units that will engage your students.

## WORKING WITH COLLEAGUES TO PLAN ACROSS GRADE LEVELS

Many schools have a committee of teachers with a representative from each grade that looks at units across a school. The purpose isn't to limit access to certain units or to create rigid unit calendars, but rather to consider children's experiences in writing as they move between the grades. These conversations can be enlightening as teachers more fully understand what happens in the grades above and below the one they teach. Matt recently worked with such a committee. They started by listing on large pieces of chart paper the units each grade was considering studying during the upcoming year. Asking "What do you notice?" led to many observations by teachers, such as:

- We notice that students study personal narrative writing in every grade, but never have a unit on fiction story writing.

- We notice that students are studying how-to writing in grades K, 1, and 2.

- We notice that students don't have as many opportunities to choose their own genre as we thought.

Until they looked at units from the experience of a child across several years, teachers didn't realize that some of these issues existed. With this knowledge, they could better coordinate units across grades and decide on any necessary changes.

If your school doesn't have a system in place for cross-grade conversation, think about ways to initiate this kind of work with a group of colleagues. You might consider bringing it up with your principal. Most principals would be receptive to a teacher who says, "I'd like to organize a group of teachers to work on making the writing experiences of our students more seamless and powerful by coordinating units from grade to grade, in ways that support our district curriculum." If you aren't receiving administrative support for this type of planning, you can still tackle it on your own by calling together a group of interested colleagues. A little bit of time invested can go a long way toward streamlining students' writing experiences.

## INSIGHTS FROM A TEACHER

Every year I anticipated that my unit on nonfiction would follow studies of illustration techniques and punctuation. However, this year I noticed that many of my students simply did not have much written on each page. They had mastered the use of various illustration techniques to add meaning into their books, and they had lots of experience expressing themselves to their readers clearly through their intentional use of punctuation. What was missing was quantity and depth. After some thought, my go-to strategy was simply to offer a new paper choice of books with more lines and less illustration space. While this motivated some of my writers to write more, I noticed that the "more" wasn't necessarily quality writing. It was at about this time when I sat down with one of my most passionate first-grade writers, Ava. Ava was always eager to try anything mentioned in a mini-lesson. She took her time on every minute detail in every illustration. Her mechanics were impeccable but she never seemed to write more than one sentence on each page.

"I have more to say. I just don't know how to make it all sound so beautiful," she said one afternoon when I invited her to add more words to her book. This was my "aha" moment. I soon found that, like Ava, other children in the class just didn't have the writing experience necessary to add rich, beautiful, descriptive language to their books. I realized that the goals of our nonfiction unit would not help my students grow in this way at this time in the year. So I decided the logical next step would be to project a unit solely on descriptive/beautiful language, and to come back to our nonfiction unit later in the year. I took some time to think through appropriate goals for this unit to help students like Ava "make it all sound so beautiful."

*—Asha Ruiz, first-grade teacher, Cincinnati*

# Naming Units

Once you've decided on a unit, you have to name it. This sounds easy, and often it is. However, coming up with a name that clearly communicates the unit's focus is important and worth some thought.

Let's say you want students to make intentional decisions about how they want their writing to sound, so you decide to teach a unit called How Authors Use Punctuation in Interesting Ways. As you study your mentor texts you notice that there are techniques beyond punctuation that impact how writing sounds, such as using bold print, all capitals, and underlining. Underlining isn't technically punctuation, so you have to decide whether to include it in your unit, especially since it's something that students will likely notice when they're studying the mentor texts. At this point, you have a couple of choices. You might decide to just stick to punctuation in this unit. Another option could be to name the unit How Authors Use Punctuation and Other Marks to Impact How Their Writing Sounds, which includes things beyond punctuation.

We're not advocating one unit name or the other. Instead, we hope you see that the name of the unit can influence what you include or leave out when projecting the unit. Naming your unit carefully helps you be clear and focused about your goals for the unit.

Regardless of what you ultimately decide to name your unit, there is something more important—which mentor texts you decide to include in your stack. We'll consider that in the next chapter.

# PROJECTING A UNIT: Mary Alice's Realistic Fiction Unit

## Deciding on a Unit

One year in early December Mary Alice was thinking about which unit of study she would start when her students came back from the holiday break. When she had created a draft calendar of units at the beginning of the year, she had tentatively planned to go into How Authors Use Punctuation in Interesting Ways, the unit she had started in January the previous year. But as the holidays grew closer she sensed that her students needed to move to a genre-specific unit as opposed to a non-genre-specific unit like punctuation. Mary Alice was contemplating a Realistic Fiction unit for several reasons:

- Her students had already been in several non-genre-specific units and she felt it was time to study a genre.

- She reviewed her district curriculum and state standards, and saw that they contained a number of goals and objectives related to writing a narrative. While she had taught some of these skills, her curriculum guides and standards were pointing her to a focused unit on writing stories.

- Mary Alice knew that she was going to study personal narratives/stories from your life toward the end of the year; because her students had experienced a number of personal narrative units in kindergarten, she thought it would be better to wait until late in the year to revisit this genre.

- She also knew that she wanted to stay away from personal narrative for now because she didn't want to do anything to diminish energy for writing. Mary Alice had a large number of very active, energetic students who, over the first several months of school, had developed a lot of energy for writing, due in part to their ability to choose their own genre. She was concerned that personal narrative might decrease their enthusiasm because students would be limited to events that had really happened to them.

- She knew that a large unit on nonfiction informational writing was coming in the spring, so she wanted to stay away from that genre.

- In reading workshop her class was completing a character study. She felt that their ability to understand characters would serve them well in a realistic fiction unit where they would need to create their own characters.

- She contemplated a study of fiction writing, but for the same reasons (a large number of highly energetic, creative writers), she felt that fictional stories might be too open and make it harder to focus on some of the craft techniques she hoped to teach.

- She had never taught this unit before and thought it would help her grow as a teacher.

So, after thinking about her long-term goals for writing, the needs of her students in this class, and the units they had already experienced or would experience later in the year, Mary Alice decided to switch from her original plan for a punctuation study, and instead embark on a unit she named Realistic Fiction: Writing Make-Believe Stories That Could Really Happen. Mary Alice filled in the title and type of unit in her projection template (Figure 4.2).

**Figure 4.2**  Mary Alice Starts Her Projection Template

## Unit of Study Projection Template

**Unit of Study:** Realistic Fiction: Writing Make Believe Stories That Could Really Happen

_____X_____ **Genre Specific**    _____ **Non-Genre Specific**    _____ **# of Weeks**

**Primary Goals**

1.

## PROJECTING A UNIT IN THE INTERMEDIATE GRADES

Realistic Fiction is a unit frequently taught in grades 3–6. The thought process for deciding on this unit is very similar to that in the primary grades. Intermediate teachers also think about the balance of genre-specific units and non-genre-specific units. Many older students are motivated by writing fictional stories (especially fantasy and science fiction), but writing fiction can be challenging since the author isn't bound by what has happened or could happen. Often intermediate teachers feel that realistic fiction provides a balance between learning about writing stories and students' desire to write some type of fiction or fantasy. Students would also have the opportunity to write other types of fiction during a non-genre-specific unit or as extra independent writing projects, but this unit would support students' need to write fiction more formally.

One fourth-grade teacher's projection template now looked like this:

**Figure 4.2**

### Unit of Study Projection Template

**Unit of Study:** *Short Stories of Realistic Fiction*

____X____ **Genre Specific**    _____ **Non-Genre Specific**    _____ **# of Weeks**

**Primary Goals**

1.

## ✎ Try It Out

1. Look at your district curricula and state standards. List the types of writing they require. List important curricular goals that are relevant to the grade level you teach.

2. Write a list including both units you have taught before and units you would like to teach, considering school expectations and professional literature.

3. Notice ways in which your unit list correlates with the standards and district curricula—reassess if you find you are missing important standards or curricular goals in your unit choices.

4. Decide which units are critical to teach this year, and which units are possibilities. In some cases, your school will have already determined critical units. See Appendix C, Critical and Possible Units of Study, for a blank template.

5. Determine a flexible sequence of units for the year, based on your school's expectations and what you know of the needs of students at your grade level.

6. Decide which unit you will plan first and use as a model as you go through the steps of the process throughout this book.

7. Name your unit and write the unit's name and type on your projection template.

# Studying a Stack of Mentor Texts and Projecting Teaching Possibilities

Once you have created your list of critical and possible units and decided on which unit to begin your year, it is time to delve a bit deeper to find the resources that can provide structure, content, and flexibility: stacks of mentor texts.

To get a better idea of the concept of studying mentor texts, we want to take you into Mary Alice's first-grade classroom. One spring, Mary Alice's students decided they wanted to make their own board games. They certainly felt they were game experts, having spent a good part of their seven years of life playing them. However, it was hard for them to articulate what kind of games they were going to make and why. With Mary Alice's guidance, they began a discussion about this. Before they started working on their own games, the children entered into a deep investigation of the games she had collected as "mentors." They read directions and noticed the common features. They looked at board design and box design. After spending time carefully examining and analyzing games, students were informed and articulate about the choices they made as they created their own games.

As with their writing, the students' finished games certainly looked and played like they were made by first graders, but after examining games through the eyes of game designers, the children created games that were close approximations of the board games you find in stores. After this unit, when students played games at home, they were able to play like game *designers* rather than just game *players*, just as students studying stacks of mentor texts are able to write from an informed perspective.

Teachers of writing understand how crucial it is for students to study real-world examples before they attempt writing on their own so that they have a vision of what they are making. Not only is it crucial for *students* to study mentor texts, this process is crucial for *teachers* projecting units of study. To prepare for projecting a unit, teachers first collect and study a stack of relevant texts, noticing characteristics and features and pulling out teaching possibilities, so that in turn they can help their students create texts inspired by the stack. This chapter will help you to both choose mentor texts and study them to create a list of teaching possibilities for your unit.

We want to make a quick clarification about mentor texts. In writing workshop the term mentor texts can be used to describe any type of text used as an example. It could be published writing, teacher generated writing, or student generated writing. During a unit of study we would use all three of these types of mentor texts in our teaching. However, when we refer to mentor texts in this book we are generally referring to *published* mentor texts.

## Why Study a Stack of Texts?

As long as you have a stack of mentor texts, you can study them and pull out relevant teaching possibilities. And conversely, if you can't find a stack of appropriate texts to study, you will find it hard to make your unit relevant for your students. Why study a type of writing for which you cannot find real-world published examples? When there are so many examples of real writing to study, it doesn't make sense to choose a genre for which there are few, if any, real-world exemplars.

As teachers, we must be able to gather and study relevant texts in order to see possibilities of what we can teach students in a particular unit of study. During this phase of the process for projecting a unit, you'll do two things:

1.  Gather and read (hopefully with colleagues) relevant mentor texts, looking for topics you could teach (based on what you know of the qualities of good writing, skills, and techniques specific to the unit's goals and your knowledge of your students).

2. Create a list of teaching possibilities (to be used later as minilessons, small-group work, and conference teaching points).

### The Importance of Using Stacks of Mentor Texts

Before we consider *how* teachers study and use a stack of texts to project a unit, let's first think about *why* this foundation for a unit is important.

There are at least three main times when teachers use a stack of mentor texts:

1. When designing a unit

2. When teaching minilessons, both during the immersion phase and throughout the unit to provide examples of authors' techniques so that students can try those things in their own writing

3. During small-group work and in individual writing conferences to provide examples for students

In many of her books, including *Study Driven*, *About the Authors*, and *Wondrous Words*, Katie Wood Ray gives compelling reasons for using a stack of texts in a classroom, both for teachers as they project and teach a unit and for student use throughout a unit. We've condensed some of that thinking in Figure 5.1.

In the next sections of this chapter, we'll explain the steps involved in using a stack of mentor texts to generate teaching possibilities for your unit, whether it's a genre-specific unit or a non-genre-specific unit. We'll discuss both gathering texts and studying them to determine what kinds of teaching possibilities they offer.

## UNITS OF STUDY THAT DON'T RELY ON STACKS OF MENTOR TEXTS

Most units of study do require mentor texts for projecting and teaching the unit, but occasionally you will encounter units that don't rely on published texts. For example, in a unit on Revision, you can use your own writing or read what published authors say about revision; you can't really see revision in published texts. Or, in a Using a Writer's Notebook unit, you can use your own notebook and read what authors say about using a notebook.

**Figure 5.1** Benefits of Using Stacks of Mentor Texts

| Benefits of Using Stacks of Mentor Texts | | |
|---|---|---|
| **Benefit** | **For Students** | **For Teachers** |
| Stacks of mentor texts provide a mental model for a genre of writing or a particular writing focus. | Immersing students in a stack of mentor texts provides a vision of the type of writing they are attempting to write themselves. | When we immerse ourselves in a stack of texts we gain a vision of the type of writing we will ask students to write, and are better able to envision teaching possibilities. |
| Stacks of mentor texts are grounded in reality and relevance. | Students are immersed in real-world examples rather than false models. | When projecting a unit based on relevant mentor texts, we ensure that the teaching possibilities we pull out are grounded in real-world examples. |
| Stacks of mentor texts help us read like writers. | As students study mentor texts they move beyond reading for enjoyment to learning new information. They take on the role of apprentice author, studying the authors' techniques and craft moves and applying them to their own writing. | We read like writers, noticing the authors' craft moves and techniques, and we read like teachers of writing, using what we know about our individual students and the teaching of writing to generate teaching possibilities that will lift the level of their writing. |
| Stacks of mentor texts expand our knowledge base. | As students are immersed in a variety of mentor texts across the year, their background knowledge about many different types of writing expands. | As we use mentor texts to project units of study, not only does our knowledge base about different types of writing grow, but our ability to fit relevant teaching possibilities with students' needs expands as well. |

# Gathering a Stack

In this section, we'll lead you through gathering the stack of texts that you'll study (and that your students will study later during the unit). So, let's get started. As you begin, ask yourself these important questions.

### What Grade Level Am I Teaching?

*Primary Grades*

In the primary grades, a stack will most likely consist of picture books, simply because that is the type of book most young students know best. Even if they have been in kindergarten for only a few weeks, they know picture books. And even if children haven't been read to regularly at home, they have seen picture books at school—and if they know what a picture book is, they can make one. Because primary children know picture books so well, that's the main kind of writing they'll make in writing workshop (Ray and Glover 2008; Ray and Cleaveland 2004). The types of picture books you choose will depend on the unit of study—picture books with a variety of illustration techniques for an illustration study, picture books with interesting punctuation for a punctuation study, and so on. Here are some ways that studying and making picture books stretch young writers.

- **Picture books allow for deeper thinking and composition.** Primary children can envision making picture books. They can't yet envision other types of writing, such as journal pages or single pieces of paper with only lines and no space for illustrations. Children compose more richly and engage in deeper thinking when they compose in picture book form. And as Katie Wood Ray shows us in her book *In Pictures and in Words* (2010), we can support children's compositional thinking in their writing by supporting their compositional thinking in their illustrations. We expect illustrations to be thoughtful, detailed compositions, not just decorations added later if there is time.

- **Young students can maintain their stamina with picture books.** When children can envision what they're making, their stamina increases. Because young children tend to have lots of experience with picture books, they have a more developed vision of what picture books look like, and therefore will work on them for longer periods of time.

- **Picture books help young students read like writers.** Making picture books makes the reading like a writer connection clear because children read picture books more intentionally when they know that they are going to make picture books themselves.

Of course, students use picture books as a springboard into more complex texts too. In second grade, we might start studying and making feature articles or book reviews. If so, students will need a stack of feature articles or book reviews to study that are appropriate for second graders.

### Intermediate Grades

In the intermediate grades, teachers have more options as they create stacks of mentor texts because students are writing many different types of text. Although intermediate-grade students could make picture books, they are more likely to write something else. They might study a stack of feature articles from magazines like *Ranger Rick* or *National Geographic for Kids* before writing their own articles. They might study short realistic fiction stories, the type you find in *Highlights* magazine. They might study commentaries, reviews, or travel articles that you find in the news-paper, in various magazines, or online. Whatever it is they're going to write, they'll need a collection of examples to study how people write it well.

Like primary students, when older students study a stack of mentor texts, they have a vision for what they will make, their thinking is richer and deeper, their stamina increases, and there is a connection between what they are reading/study-ing and what they are making. Because the benefits are the same for students, both primary and intermediate teachers need to study a stack of texts before projecting most units of study.

## Where Can I Find Appropriate Texts for My Stack?

One of the most frequent questions we get is, "Where do I find texts for my stack?" The prospect of coming up with enough texts that will support a unit of study can seem a bit daunting. It does take some time, but fortunately it's not as hard as it seems. In the primary grades, you'll probably be looking for picture books, and in the intermediate grades you'll generally want other types of texts.

### Primary Grades

In the primary grades, you first need to decide if your unit will be genre-specific or non-genre-specific. For example, will you be looking for great examples of memoirs for a memoir study (genre specific)? Will you be looking for picture books with interesting illustration techniques for an illustration study (not genre specific)? The focus of your unit will determine the common characteristics of the texts you will pull together for the stack.

Once you know clearly what you're looking for, the easiest place to start is in your own classroom library of picture books. The advantage to starting with books in your classroom is that you already know them well. You'll be surprised how many of these books can fit into various units of study. You can supplement your classroom library with material from the school library, media center, or your local library or bookstore.

There are also plenty of lists of mentor texts available. You'll find references to possible mentor texts in many professional books on writing. Our favorite resource for the primary grades is *About the Authors* (2004), in which Katie Wood Ray and Lisa Cleaveland describe specific units of study and provides a good starter list of mentor texts for many of them. A Google search will also generate numerous lists. However, we always caution teachers to take other people's lists with a grain of salt. A book on a list for someone else's unit of study may not fit with your unit's goals. Or it might not be a book you particularly enjoy. Since the challenge in most units is to narrow down your stack to a manageable number, you'll want to consider carefully what to include and leave out, rather than just adding a book because it's on someone's list.

## GET TO KNOW YOUR CLASSROOM LIBRARY

We often encourage teachers to gather their favorite books from their classroom and study them as a teacher of writers. Ask yourself, "Which books offer lots of opportunities to teach something about writing?" It's a great way to both get to know what resources you already have available, and to practice deeply engaging with the content as a teacher of writers.

### Intermediate Grades

In the intermediate grades, since you're less likely to use picture books (unless students will be making picture books), you won't as often start your search with a list of possible mentor texts. What's more helpful is to have some ideas about where to look for mentor texts. One example, *Highlights* magazine (thanks to Carl Anderson for this suggestion), is a great source for short realistic fiction. However, it's not very helpful if we tell you specifically that you must go out and find the October 2006 issue of *Highlights*. What is helpful is to know that *Highlights* is a great resource—and there are many others: *American Girl, Boys' Life, Story Works, Cricket,* and so on. It's fairly easy to get a stack of this kind of magazine from parents or your local library (or ask your doctor's office to save them).

A wonderful resource for finding stacks of mentor texts for both the primary and intermediate grades is Katie Wood Ray's book *Study Driven*. In it Katie gives a brief description of more than twenty units, with key points to consider for each unit of study. She then points you in the right direction for finding places to look for stacks for each unit.

Increasingly, some teachers look to the Internet for texts. The Internet can be a wonderful tool, and can make it easy to search quickly for a particular text. It's important, however, to make sure that texts you find online look like what your students will be writing and also resemble what you might find in a magazine. It's important that mentor texts provide examples of exactly what you'll be asking students to do—and unless you are asking students to write digital texts, the texts they study should not have features specific to digital texts. There are numerous online resources that can be useful, as long as you look at them with a critical eye.

### How Do I Decide Which Texts to Include in My Stack?

Once you've found a variety of sources for mentor texts, it's important to be thoughtful about which ones to include. The more each text has to offer in terms of teaching possibilities, the stronger your unit will be. Here are some questions to ask yourself as you ponder what to include.

- **Can I use the text for several different teaching points?** There are advantages to having students get to know a small collection of texts well, as opposed to getting to know a larger stack more superficially. If we're going to use a text multiple times throughout a unit, it needs to have several potential teaching points. For example, the memoir "Teeth" found in Ralph Fletcher's book *Marshfield Dreams* is packed with potential teaching points for a unit on memoir. In it Ralph has just a bit of dialogue, uses strong verbs, shows his internal thinking, and has a sense of distance and reflection, to name a few. All of these teaching points could be used as springboards for minilessons.

- **Do I need to keep an eye out for a particular crafting element or feature?** If there's a particular technique or element you want to show your students, you'll need to ensure that it's present somewhere in your mentor texts. For example, recently a teacher realized that in her stack of all-about/informational books, none of them had a table of contents. Since she wanted her students to consider including a table of contents, she added a couple of books that had them.

- **If I'm collecting a genre-specific stack, is this text a clear example of the genre?** Some texts fall into a gray area in terms of genre. For example, there is a gray area between personal essays and commentaries. Some essays feel like commentaries and some commentaries have more of an essay feel. When building a stack for either unit, it's best to avoid texts that are ambiguous and instead choose really clear examples of the genre. Of course, you could use a gray-area text and have students debate why it does or does not fit in a particular genre. But generally you'll want most of your texts to be clear examples of the genre.

- **Will this text engage my students?** While the content of the text isn't crucial, you want stacks with examples that students will enjoy reading and find interesting and engaging regardless of topic. For example, if you are coordinating a literary nonfiction picture book unit of study with an animal research project in science, you wouldn't have to choose only animal books for your writing lessons. The topic doesn't affect what you are going to teach students about writing.

- **How many books/texts should be in a stack?** We often hear from teachers that they are concerned about where they will find all of these books or texts. Fortunately, you probably don't need as many as you think. Even though you might initially collect fifteen to twenty texts, you will need only five to eight texts that you know well that will be the basis of your minilessons. The remaining books should be available for the first few days as students immerse themselves in the unit, but you shouldn't feel as if you need to teach from that bigger stack. As we noted earlier, we find that it's better to have a few texts that you know really well than a large stack you know superficially. You also don't need a new text for each minilesson. It's more powerful, and time efficient, to come back to a text students already know and draw their attention to something new that the author has done well.

## USING MENTOR TEXTS FROM THE STACK DURING CONFERENCES

Having some books you know really well helps during writing conferences. As Carl Anderson (2009) and others remind us, using a mentor text during a writing conference helps ensure that we are teaching the writer, not the writing, by showing students how they can try a skill they've seen a published author use. Sometimes teachers ask Matt how he happens to have just the right book available during a conference. They believe he must know a wide variety of books really well. He actually doesn't—Matt knows lots of books fairly well, and he knows *some* books *really* well. Both Matt and Mary Alice have a smaller set of books that they know inside and out (books that may fit well in several different stacks throughout the year) so they can pull them out in a conference and quickly show a student a particular technique.

- **Is this a text that I might be able to use in more than one unit?** Some texts can be used in multiple units, so we're more likely to include those in our stack. For example, we might read a personal essay early in the year in fifth grade as part of a genre overview, knowing that we'll use it again later in the year in a personal essay study. We have several books that travel between stacks throughout the year. For example, *Roller Coaster* by Marla Frazee travels between the following unit stacks: Launching Writing Workshop, Where Writers Get Ideas, Illustration Study, Reading Like a Writer, and How Authors Use Punctuation in Interesting Ways. We certainly use books that are relevant for only one stack, but we each have a collection of favorites that we use in different units throughout the year.

- **How do I collect stacks for non-genre-specific units?** A stack of mentor texts is as important for a non-genre-specific unit. What's tricky is that there are some non-genre specific units that don't have a stack (revision, how to have better peer conferences, etc.) and some that do. However, many teachers struggle with a stack for the ones that do, and tend to think that non-genre specific units don't have a stack. The key is to make sure that these stacks are actually non-genre-specific. Here's what we mean. Let's say you've decided to study Where Authors Find Ideas in either the primary or intermediate grades. In this stack of mentor texts we might include *Owl Babies* by Martin Waddell and *In My New Yellow Shirt* by Eileen Spinelli because they both have great author's notes that tell us where the author got the idea for the book. *Owl Babies* is the story of three baby owls waiting for their mother to return to the nest. It's a story book (a book about a time something happened), whereas *In My New Yellow Shirt* is a list book. In this book a boy receives a yellow shirt for his birthday; each page shows him pretending to be something yellow (a canary, a taxi, a lion). This book is organized as a list, not a story. By including both story books and list books you keep your stack non-genre-specific—but both choices provide examples of where authors find ideas.

  Let's look at an intermediate example. In a genre overview (designed to help students consider different genre possibilities), you could collect a stack that includes a how-to article, a persuasive essay, a fictional story, a memoir, a review, a biographical sketch, and some poems. A stack of texts like this would help students see that they could create many different types of writing, including but not limited to stories.

Sometimes teachers inadvertently include only picture books or texts that are stories. By including only stories in a non-genre-specific unit the teacher is unintentionally communicating that the child should only be writing stories. Therefore, it's good to check that your texts for non-genre-specific units represent a variety of genres.

● **Who's right? How do I decide where a text fits?** We believe that teachers must decide for themselves whether or not a certain text fits in a stack. It is important to be able to articulate why you've included the books in your stack—and teachers collecting texts for the same unit are likely to make different decisions. Over the years, we've asked a handful of literacy experts, all of whom we admire greatly, if they would include the book *Wemberly Worried* by Kevin Henkes in their mentor texts for a unit on realistic fiction. (If you know Kevin's books *Chrysanthemum* or *Lily's Purple Plastic Purse*, then you can picture *Wemberly Worried*, the story of a mouse who worries about everything, including her first day of school.)

Some said they would and others said they wouldn't. They were split down the middle. Those who *would* use it said it has great crafting techniques and that it's an engaging story that young children relate to. Those who *wouldn't* use it pointed to the fact that Wemberly is a mouse (so how can it be realistic fiction?). Those who *would* use it replied that the story itself is absolutely realistic. After all, if you couldn't see the pictures, you would never know that Wemberly is a mouse. Those who *wouldn't* use it said something like, "Why use a book that might cause some confusion with students when there are other good realistic fiction books that don't have talking animals? Something like *How to Heal a Broken Wing* by Bob Graham." Both groups of experts had rationales for why they would or wouldn't use the book.

There isn't a right or wrong answer to whether or not *Wemberly Worried* belongs in a stack of realistic fiction. It is more important to be thoughtful about what to include and what to leave out, since what's in your stack will impact what students notice and try out in their writing. As always, we're as (or more) interested in how a teacher's thinking supports her decisions as we are in what books she chooses to include. Over time we are developing the skill of looking critically at books, which won't happen if we rely on someone else's list.

Depending on the unit, it may be difficult to ensure that each mentor text has examples of everything you want to teach, especially the first time you create a stack for a unit. Fortunately, you can refine and strengthen your stack each year. If the mentor texts have many of the characteristics you are hoping to teach, they will be more useful in supporting your teaching. Your goals for the unit and what you most want your students to do will impact your choices.

# Studying Your Texts and Noticing Teaching Possibilities

Now that you have decided which mentor texts to include in your stack, the next step is to study them and notice what the authors have done to craft these texts. Hopefully you can do this with a group of colleagues. You'll need to read both like a writer and like a teacher of writers. Here's the difference between the two:

- *Reading like a writer:* The teacher first engages with the text as though she were going to write something like it herself. She notices and names all of the techniques, features, and craft moves the author has used.

- *Reading like a teacher of writing:* After the teacher notices and names what the writer has done, she narrows her focus to consider which of these items her students might notice, or which items she might point out that her students could try. She keeps her grade level and her particular students' needs in mind, while also considering schoolwide goals for student writing.

To illustrate the difference: When studying a realistic fiction stack as a *writer*, a first-grade teacher notices that the authors do some foreshadowing by mentioning a detail that will be important later in the story. As a *teacher*, she notices this technique but decides that it's not one her first graders are ready for. When you're reading like an adult writer, you notice everything, but when you're reading like a teacher of writers, you factor in all that you know about your individual students and about the teaching of writing at your grade level.

## Reading Like a Writer

As you start studying a stack you first want to read like a writer. Immerse yourself in the books and get to know them well. If you are projecting a genre-specific study, you'll be getting to know that particular genre. If you are projecting a non-genre-specific unit, you will be familiarizing yourself with the connections between the texts as well as studying each piece individually. As you read, pay attention to all the author has done to craft this text. It can be helpful to take notes as you go, keeping in mind that not everything you notice will work for your students. Consider the organization of the text, crafting techniques the author used, language, features of the particular type of text, and so forth.

When we read with a writer's eye, we expand the range of potential teaching points for minilessons and conferences later on. Invariably, whenever we think that none of our students will try a technique we noticed in a text, one of them does. But we can't teach everything, so reading like a writer helps us build a broad range of observations about a text.

For example, let's say you were studying picture books for an illustration study in second grade. You might notice that illustrators sometimes show a bird's-eye view, like in *Dylan's Day Out* by Peter Catalanato or *Hoptoad* by Jane Yolen. However, you might think that a bird's-eye view is too sophisticated a technique for your students. But you might be surprised, as we were recently in a second-grade class: A student noticed this technique as we were looking at a picture book and tried it out. See what Olivia did on this page of her book about swim lessons (Figure 5.2).

Reading like a writer ourselves helps expand what we know about the texts so that we are better prepared to support students as they notice techniques and try them out.

The next step, reading like a teacher of writers, helps us envision curriculum and teaching possibilities for our specific students. (Numerous resources discuss the importance of reading like a writer and the particulars of how to get better at it. See Appendix E for a selection.)

**Figure 5.2** Olivia Tries Out a Bird's-Eye View

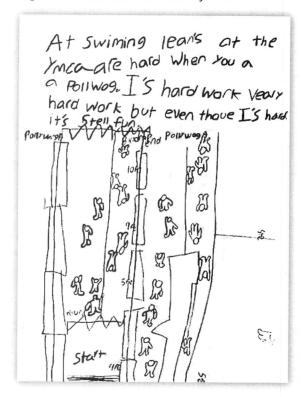

## Reading Like a Teacher of Writers

Now that you have observed an author's technique as a writer, you will want to put your teacher hat back on, think about your classroom and your students, and read like a *teacher of writers*. Think about what your students might notice on their own, what they need help noticing, and what they might try in their own writing.

As you look for teaching possibilities in your stack, keep your particular students in mind by asking yourself some questions.

- What is the range of skills of the writers in my class?
- What will I need to be able to show both my most experienced and my least experienced writers?
- What skills and techniques have been challenging for my students this year?
- What skills and techniques will stretch my students' thinking?

As you study your stack using this lens, write down teaching possibilities (which will eventually become the basis for minilessons and conferences). We don't recommend writing them on your planning sheet yet since this list is more of a first draft: everything you could teach your particular group of students in this unit, rather than a focused list. There will be time to narrow it down later, so you don't want to eliminate anything yet. You also don't need to worry about grouping similar ideas, or figuring out which teaching points will come early or late in the unit. That will come later as well.

By capturing all of the teaching possibilities you see in your stack, you will end up with a much longer list of teaching points than you will have time to teach in this unit. That's okay; actually it's exactly what you want right now. Even if a teaching possibility doesn't "make the cut" of being a minilesson topic on your final projection template, you still want to have it in your bank of possibilities as a conference or minilesson topic should it become relevant as the unit progresses.

### Studying Stacks with Colleagues

We find it particularly helpful to study texts with a group of teachers. Invariably one teacher will notice something that other teachers miss. And then, that new item opens up other possibilities to study. Here's an example. Matt and Mary Alice have studied the picture book *Bat Loves the Night* by Nicola Davies with teachers in workshop settings. Teachers spend time noticing the numerous crafting techniques and then share with the group what they found. Invariably someone will mention the ellipsis followed by a period on page 15 and there will be a short conversation about this interesting punctuation. Then, without

## READING LIKE A TEACHER OF WRITERS: NOTICING TEACHING POSSIBILITIES IN A STACK OF TEXTS

But what do you look for when compiling a list of teaching possibilities? This can seem daunting, especially if you are new to studying mentor texts in this way, or if you are projecting a unit of study you've never taught before. Fortunately, the more you study texts the better you get at noticing features and techniques. It certainly helps to study with colleagues, because they will see teaching possibilities that you don't, and vice versa. You will notice more as a group than you will individually. You'll also find that once you spot a particular technique in one text, you'll start noticing it in other texts as well. For example, in a unit on text structures, a second-grade teacher might notice that books with an obvious text pattern usually have an ending that breaks the pattern to bring the book to a close. Once you've noticed that in one text, you can't help but see it in others.

As you begin to notice and jot down teaching possibilities, it can be helpful to consider the aspects of writing we list below. This certainly isn't meant to be an all-encompassing list—there are many resources designed to help you learn more about crafting techniques, the qualities of good writing, and the processes that writers use (see Appendices D and E for a sampling). But this list can provide a framework to spark your ideas.

- Think about the qualities of good writing. There are many lists of the qualities of good writing, but most of them are fairly similar. Consider the following qualities in the texts you are studying.
    - ✦ Organization
    - ✦ Details
    - ✦ Voice
    - ✦ Conventions
    - ✦ Meaning
- Think about the process an author would go through to create a text in this stack. You might consider these questions:
    - ✦ What is the purpose of this type of writing?
    - ✦ How do authors find topics?

*continues*

✦ Who is the audience for this writing?

✦ What type of prewriting do authors need to do to plan a text like this?

● Notice the beginnings and endings of the text.

● What type of graphic support, if any, does this stack contain?

● How might you support students in finding topics for this unit? Is there any evidence of where these authors found their topics?

● What conventions and editing teaching points do you see?

● What type of revision (adding, deleting, changing, moving) might this stack lend itself to the most?

● What types of punctuation do you see?

● What crafting techniques do you notice?

● What strikes you the most about this text?

● What do you notice in this stack that is different from other stacks you've studied?

prompting, the teachers start to look back through the book searching for other punctuation, especially if they hadn't been thinking about punctuation the first time through.

This type of building on each other's thinking is common in groups. What's particularly helpful about this phenomenon is that after studying a stack with a group, you will have expanded your own repertoire of possible teaching points. The more you study texts, the more you'll know about writing. And the more you study a stack with colleagues, the wider your scope of possibilities will be.

### Beyond Studying a Stack: Additional Ways to Generate Teaching Possibilities

Here are two more strategies you can use to help you project a unit and be prepared to support your students. We don't build these strategies into our projection template but it can be helpful to have additional strategies in mind. Katie Wood Ray has been using both of these strategies in her work with teachers.

## INSIGHTS FROM A COACH

One of the greatest successes that I have had as an instructional coach is when I planned a historical fiction unit of study with our fifth-grade team. They were giving up their forty-five-minute prep time to plan the unit and hoped to have it finished by the end of the period. When I showed up with magazines and excerpts from historical fiction books to read through for "noticings," the body language from the team was less than favorable. Let's just say that I wish I had a quarter for every time they looked at the clock.

However, once they delved into the literature and realized all the great teaching points for their minilessons, it became very easy to create goals for their students' writing. After the goals were written, the minilesson ideas began to flow with a great synergy. Although we weren't finished in forty-five minutes, the teachers agreed to meet after school to complete the unit. A couple of days later, each one came back to me individually and said that because we began the process with the mentor texts, they were better able to understand the process for writing a unit and thus more effectively teach writing to their students.

—*Theresa Haler, Instructional Coach, Indianapolis*

### Create Your Own Writing to Use with Students

You will likely use your own writing as a tool for teaching. However, the advantages of creating your own version of what students will be making go beyond just being able to model reading like a writer. Creating your own texts also helps you better understand the process that authors go through, which in turn will help you help your students understand this process.

For example, when you create your own memoir you go through the process of being a memoir writer. You better understand the need to find a topic of personal meaning and can share with students the process you used to find your topic. As you work to show the sense of distance in your memoir, you are actually using the process you want your students to use.

### Consider Notebook Work for the Intermediate Grades

As you project a unit in the intermediate grades it might be helpful to consider what type of work students will be doing in their writer's notebooks at various points in the unit. We know some teachers who add a column to their projecting template and describe what kind of notebook work students will do each day.

For example, a group of teachers recently projected a unit called How-to Writing. Here are some of the ideas they had for notebook work during the unit.

- Students will read their notebook entries looking for topics that they know a lot about and could teach someone else.

- Students will create a list of possible how-to topics in their notebook and put stars next to items they might want to try.

- Students will use their notebook to experiment with a potential topic by writing everything they can think of about their topic on a new page in their notebook.

- In their notebooks students will start a list of tips and warnings for their reader.

Selecting a stack takes some time, but once you assemble your mentor texts, you are well on your way to projecting an effective unit. With these texts and your list of teaching possibilities, you are ready to determine essential and secondary goals for your unit.

# PROJECTING A UNIT OF STUDY:
## Mary Alice's Realistic Fiction Unit

### Gathering a Stack of Texts

Mary Alice's first step was to decide what books she wanted in her stack of realistic fiction texts. She knew her stack would be composed of picture books (rather than short stories from magazines like *Highlights*, *American Girl*, or *Boys' Life*) because picture books were what her students (like most first graders) were most familiar with, and picture books would provide students with a vision for what they could make. They had read tons of picture books, and Mary Alice knew that her students would compose better texts if they were also thoughtful in the composition of their illustrations.

Mary Alice didn't contemplate using chapter books, even though many of her first graders were reading them. Chapter books simply didn't match the length of what her students would be writing.

But narrowing her list down to realistic fiction picture books wasn't enough. She knew that between her classroom and the school library, there were hundreds of realistic fiction picture books her students would enjoy. She started asking herself several questions, based in part on what she had read in professional books about writing realistic fiction.

- *What is the character's age?* Was she going to use primarily picture books where the main characters are children, about the same age as her students, or books in which the characters are adults, or a mixture?

- *Is there a clear problem and solution?* Would she use primarily picture books that have a clear problem and solution, like *The Ticky Tacky Doll* (the story of a girl who has to leave her deeply loved doll behind when school begins), or would she include books that aren't so explicit, like Dav Pilkey's *The Paperboy* (a story of a boy delivering newspapers)?

- *Should the books be written in first person or third?* Would she include realistic fiction books that are written in first person, like *Owl Moon* by Jane Yolen? Or would she include only books written in third person?

- *Do the books show multiple failed attempts at a solution?* She knew some teachers limited their stacks to realistic fiction stories where the main character makes several failed attempts to solve a problem before finding a solution that works. She could limit her stack to those books, include some of them, or decide not to include any of them.

After considering these options, she decided what to keep in her stack and what to leave out. She decided to use mainly books that were written in third person because she wanted her students to broaden their choice of characters; up until that point they had mostly been writing in first person. She decided to leave in *Owl Moon* even though it's written in first person because it's a book she loves, and it has many crafting techniques she wanted her students to try out. She also chose books that have a clear problem and solution as she felt they might help students organize their writing. However, she avoided using only books where the character makes multiple attempts before finding a solution as these might be overly formulaic and limit what her students could do. Finally, she decided to use primarily books in which the main characters are children because she felt it would be easier for her students to create stories with children as the main characters.

Here are some of the books she kept in her stack:

*How to Heal a Broken Wing*, Bob Graham

*The Ticky Tacky Doll*, Cynthia Rylant

*I Want a Dog*, Helga Bansch

*"The Trouble with Dogs . . . " Said Dad*, Bob Graham

*Peter's Chair*, Ezra Jack Keats

*Goggles*, Ezra Jack Keats

*Owl Moon*, Jane Yolen

Even though she settled on these rough parameters for her stack, she didn't rule out straying from them a bit during the unit. She also knew she would have to decide how much to require her students to adhere to these parameters. On the one hand, she knew that these guidelines would help her students focus more on the quality of the writing. But she also wanted to be careful not to reduce their energy and motivation for writing. She knew that she would have to consider the individual student regarding decisions on how "realistic" a story needed to be, or her definition of characters "about" the same age as the writer. Regardless of those individual decisions, she was confident that her stack would provide students with a vision of what they could make with numerous techniques they could notice and try out.

## Studying a Stack for Teaching Possibilities

Once Mary Alice and her colleagues had selected their mentor texts, they got together one morning before school to study them. They spread the books out on a table and started reading them as teachers of writing, looking for techniques their students might notice or that the teachers might point out. They had fifteen to twenty books, so they also began thinking about which five to eight books they would use over and over in the units, and which ones they might use on occasion.

As they started to read through their stack they each started a list of techniques they wanted students to learn. They didn't try to limit their lists or debate which techniques were best for their students. At this point they didn't want to rule anything out; they knew they could narrow it down later. They wanted to imagine all that students might try.

They also considered what process these authors might have gone through that their students could learn from. For example, they noticed in one author's notes that the story was based on a real experience, and thought that their students might try using a real experience to create their fictional stories.

After studying their stack for about forty-five minutes they had a pretty good list of teaching possibilities. Figure 5.3 shows Mary Alice's list.

**Figure 5.3** Mary Alice's Initial Jotted List of Teaching Possibilities

Realistic Fiction

- Some have dialogue, some not
- Some have problem stated as opening line or problem is revealed almost immediately
- Some have more set up before problem - setting, character devel.,
- Some show setting only in illustrations - not in text
- Some describe setting in words and text
- show passage of time - sometimes in illustrations, sometimes in words, sometimes both
- internal thought
- character feelings show on faces in illustrations
- some show how character feels
- some tell how character feels
- use detailed list to move from general detail to specific details
- some have one problem, one solution
- some have one problem, multiple attempts at solving
- use a variety of dialogue markers, not just said
- punctuation - helps reader understand character - shows how character said the words
- use of metaphors and similes
- use of italics to show what people are saying/thinking
-

**Figure 5.4** Mary Alice's Sticky Notes

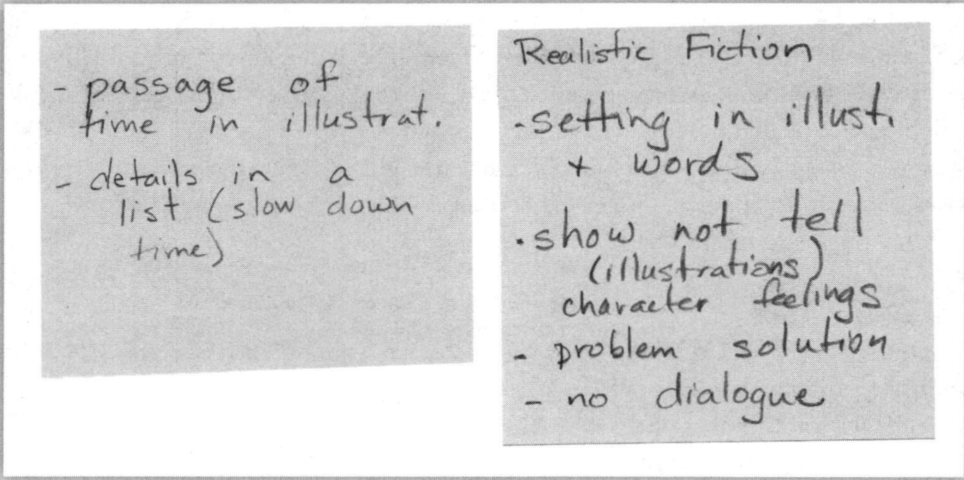

You'll notice that the list isn't organized in any particular way; she simply wanted to capture their thinking about what they noticed in the stack.

Mary Alice often writes her noticings on sticky notes (see Figure 5.4) so she can then put them right in her picture books. This allows her to quickly find specific techniques that she wants to show her students, especially during writing conferences.

## PROJECTING A UNIT IN THE INTERMEDIATE GRADES

### Gathering a Stack of Texts

Deciding what to include in your stack is a little different in the intermediate grades due the larger range of possibilities. In the intermediate grades we want to make sure that what we are reading/studying is about the same length as what students would write. Not exactly, but approximately. For example, we wouldn't include novels and chapter books, since they are much longer than what students would write. We also wouldn't use an excerpt from a chapter book, unless it was a short stand-alone story that didn't need the rest of book to be understood.

We typically coordinate our realistic fiction units in writing and reading by starting the reading unit a week or two before the writing unit. In a reading unit in the intermediate grades, we use chapter books at a variety of reading levels, but we need different books for a writing unit—texts that more closely match what students would write.

One option for this unit is to use short stories of realistic fiction, the kind you find in children's magazines such as *Highlights, American Girl, Boys' Life,* and *Cricket*. Depending on the grade we might use more stories from a magazine like *Highlights*, which tend to be shorter, or from *American Girl*, which tend to be longer. In this stack we might also pull selections from a collection of short stories.

Another option is to study picture books. Realistic fiction picture books can be very complex and written at a high level; using them doesn't mean lowering the level of the writing. If we decide to create a stack of picture books, we have to consider how much time to spend thinking about composing with illustrations. Because picture books use both pictures and words to compose meaning, our fourth graders will need to consider both. Even short stories from children's magazines have illustrations, and while they're not nearly as crucial in composing meaning, we need to consider how to include illustration support for the stories our students write.

In the intermediate grades we generally use a stack of five to eight short stories from children's magazines because they match up well in terms of length and complexity. They allow students to have a good sense of the wholeness of story and contain many of the techniques and features we want children to try out in this unit.

## Studying a Stack for Teaching Possibilities

In the intermediate grades the process of pulling out teaching possibilities is very similar to that for the primary grades, and while the exact items are more sophisticated, the list simply represents what teachers notice. Teachers also start thinking about possibilities for what students will do in their writer's notebooks during the unit. See the following box for a typical list of teaching possibilities for a fourth-grade realistic fiction unit. This list is a composite based on our recent conversations and interactions with intermediate-grade teachers. It was generated by studying realistic fiction published in various children's magazines

## SAMPLE FOURTH-GRADE INITIAL TEACHING POSSIBILITIES

- Bits of dialogue but not too much
- Lead that engages the reader
- Some stories start with dialogue
- Some stories start with a description or action
- Written in scenes
- Author skips ahead in time rather than writing everything that happened/only includes important scenes
- Well organized—clear beginning, series of events, end
- Clear problem and solution
- Usually a change in character emotions
- Sometimes author tells how a character is feeling
- Sometimes the author shows rather than tells how a character is feeling
- Often use dialogue or internal thinking to show emotions
- Describe specific actions
- Engaging title
- All have at least a couple of illustrations
- Many use examples to show character traits
- Author creates a setting
- Author sets the reader up early on to understand the character, setting, etc.
- Some have an unexpected ending
- Some use foreshadowing by including something early on that becomes important later

**Try It Out**

You have decided on and named the unit you are going to project. The next step is to gather and study your stack of mentor texts.

1. Gather a large stack of texts (around fifteen) that you might use in this unit.

2. Read through the stack as a writer, noticing everything you can about what the writer is doing.

3. Read through the stack as a teacher of writers, keeping your eyes open for particularly good examples to use with students based on what you know of your students and the qualities of good writing. (See Appendices D and E.)

4. List all of the teaching possibilities that you envision from this stack.

5. Decide on five to eight texts that will provide the foundation for your study. These are texts that you feel contain the richest examples of teaching possibilities.

# Determining Primary and Secondary Goals

After studying a stack of texts and creating a list of teaching possibilities, it's tempting to start projecting how the minilessons will unfold. But before you start projecting minilesson topics, you need to make decisions regarding the unit's priorities. Creating clear goals gives the unit direction and helps you articulate to yourself and your students the desired outcomes for the unit.

Goals are important for any type of endeavor. Whether you're starting a new job or starting a new diet, goals provide direction and motivation for what you want to accomplish. Now that you've studied your stack of mentor texts and listed teaching possibilities, you have a sense of what you want students to be able to learn and do in this unit. You're ready to set unit goals. In projecting a unit of study we generally look at two types of unit goals: *primary goals* and *secondary goals*. Primary goals are broader, big-picture goals for the unit, while secondary goals are more specific and focused.

Before we look at unit goals, it is important to realize that there are larger, long-term goals that impact every unit of study. We can think of these as *lifetime goals* for writers since they cut across grades and units. They describe what we want students to be able to do as writers when they leave elementary school or high school. Many authors have shared such a list. Here are some of our long-term goals for writers.

- Students should enjoy writing. Writing should be seen as a meaningful, rewarding endeavor.

- Students should find real purposes and audiences for which to write.

- Students should be able to communicate clearly and effectively through writing.

- Students should be able to engage in a process of inquiry to read like a writer: to notice techniques and skills that authors use and then try them in their own writing.

Goals like these apply to every unit of study and will permeate all of the work we do with students. You will have your own list of long-term goals that guide your work. Because these perennial goals influence our thinking for all units, we don't include them in our goals for individual units.

# Primary Goals

Primary goals are broad, overarching goals that describe the big things we want students to learn in a unit. There are several ways to think about primary goals.

- Primary goals describe what we want students to be able to do at the end of the unit (and henceforth in their writing) that they can't do at the start.

- Primary goals describe what most minilessons in the unit will build toward. For example, a primary goal for a punctuation study could be, "Students will show evidence of intentionally using punctuation to impact how their writing sounds." With that goal in place almost every minilesson works toward that goal. If only a chunk of minilessons will be focused on a goal, then it's probably a secondary goal.

- Primary goals should provide an overarching "umbrella" focus for the unit.

Deciding on primary goals is sometimes more difficult than it appears. It's often easier to think of very specific goals as opposed to broader goals that capture big ideas. As our friend and editor Zoë Ryder White says, "One has to find the sweet spot where the goal is broad enough to express something larger that we want kids to come away with, but specific enough so that it doesn't become a catch-all that could apply to any unit." Fortunately, primary goals are easier to create if we keep the following considerations in mind:

1. *Limit the number of primary goals.* Because these are broad, overarching goals, we usually create one to three. If we have five or six primary goals, then they're probably not all the most important. Everything can't be of primary importance, and having too many goals takes you in too many different directions.

2. *When creating primary goals, make sure they are action-oriented.* Instruction is clarified when we write action-oriented goals. Goals that state "students will understand . . . " or "students will notice . . . " are more like reading goals than writing goals, and they don't specify what we hope students will be able to *do* as writers. This passively phrased goal for an informational all-about book study—"Students will notice and identify various nonfiction text features"—can be tweaked so that it moves beyond simply noticing and identifying and asks students to use some of those text features in their writing. By rewording the goal as, "Students will notice multiple nonfiction text features and use them in their writing," it becomes a writing goal.

3. *Return to your sources when creating primary goals.* There are two main sources for primary goals: state standards/district curricula and the list of teaching possibilities you collected while studying your mentor texts. Many teachers find it helpful to have their standards or curriculum open when they start creating a unit. District curricula and state standards can be a starting point for primary goals. They probably won't provide the specific goals you need, but they can often be modified for your unit. Here are some questions to ask yourself while reviewing the state, district, and Common Core standards:

   ● Which standards will be met by the unit I am projecting?

   ● If this is a genre-specific unit, which type of writing (narrative, informative/explanatory, opinion) could I focus on in this unit? Are the Common Core goals for certain types of writing possible unit goals?

   ● How could technology enhance my unit, since the Common Core requires students to write using technology at certain grades?

   ● Are there places I might incorporate research into my unit (knowing that research isn't a prerequisite), since the Common Core and many state standards require students to do research as part of writing?

   ● How will I focus on revision in this unit?

   ● How might I incorporate a variety of writing experiences for a range of tasks, purposes, and audiences?

   As you're creating primary unit goals, think about the teaching possibilities you noticed when studying your stack of mentor texts. Individual items on the list probably won't be primary goals, but look for patterns and groupings, which can lead to broader ideas. Here are some questions to ask yourself while you are examining your list of teaching possibilities:

- Why did I decide to teach this unit?
- Why did I decide to teach this unit at this time?
- Which items on the list are specific to this particular unit of study, as opposed to items that could show up in multiple units of study?
- If it's a genre-specific unit, which items help distinguish this genre from others?
- If it's a non-genre-specific unit, which items describe the core characteristic of this study?
- Which items are the most important to me, based on what I know about writing and what I know about my specific class of students?

4. *Primary goals are grade specific.* We would expect different primary goals for a particular unit in different grades. Primary goals for a second-grade unit on informational/all-about writing should be more sophisticated than those for kindergarten students in the same unit. In second grade a primary goal might be, "Students will use multiple text features that they have noticed in mentor texts." In kindergarten a primary goal might be, "Students will write texts that teach the reader facts about a topic." Or, imagine an intermediate unit on writing reviews. A fifth-grade goal could be, "Students will write a review that shares an opinion based on both the positive and negative things about the topic being reviewed." In third grade, a primary goal for the same unit might be, "Students will notice, formulate, and share an opinion in writing." Looking at unit goals for other grade levels can help you think about goals for your own grade, but they will need to be modified.

5. *Consider the experience of your students when creating primary goals.* You also need to consider what experience your students have with this type of writing. If this is a totally new type of writing or a new unit for them, the primary goals will be less sophisticated than if students had extensive experience with this type of writing in previous years, or even practice from earlier in the school year. In some units one of the primary goals could simply state that students will do the type of writing described in the name of the unit. For example, a primary goal in a kindergarten poetry unit could be, "Students will produce writing that looks and sounds like a poem." Basically this simply says that students will write poems, which

## EXAMPLES OF PRIMARY GOALS

As always, we're not suggesting you use these actual goals for your students. We provide them just to give you a sense of the scope, breadth, and language of primary goals.

- Primary goal for a Genre Overview study in first grade: "Students will be able to articulate what type of book they are going to make (identify their genre) before they start."

- Primary goal for a Text Structure study in second grade: "Students will show evidence of using an obvious text structure when creating a book."

- Primary goal for a Realistic Fiction study in fourth grade: "Students will write stories that include different types of details (dialogue, actions, etc.) to show character emotions."

seems obvious since that's the unit of study. But if you're a kindergartner and you've never written a poem before, that's a pretty significant goal.

However, that goal might not be appropriate for second-grade students who wrote poems in kindergarten and first grade. They would need a more sophisticated goal, such as, "Students will show evidence of trying out several types of figurative language." But if the second graders have never written poems before, the primary goal would be less sophisticated.

Of course, the same thing is true in upper grades. If your fifth graders have never written a feature article, then producing an article that engages and informs (Ray 2006) could be one of the primary goals. However, if the students wrote a feature article in the previous year, producing just one wouldn't be demanding enough. The level of experience combined with the age of the students determines the sophistication of the primary goals.

## Secondary Goals

While primary goals describe broad, overarching aims for the unit, secondary goals focus on specific skills, techniques, and outcomes and encompass the total development of the child as a writer. Secondary goals generally focus on these areas:

- Qualities of good writing
- Writing habits

- Building a community of writers
- Revision
- Editing and conventions

When writing secondary goals it's important to consider how long you plan to spend on each topic. Secondary goals usually describe a *chunk* of minilessons in a unit rather than just the topic for one day. If you've written a goal for a topic you plan to spend just one day on, it's probably not broad enough to be considered a secondary goal.

That said, there are times when a secondary goal might require only a minilesson or two. Sometimes secondary goals describe a focus for the unit that you may introduce in one minilesson and then follow up on in conferences throughout the unit. And on rare occasions, you may have a secondary goal with no minilessons attached to it because the goal is a by-product of the broader unit goals.

To see how these scenarios play out, let's consider a primary Illustration unit of study. One secondary goal might be that students include setting details in their illustrations and writing. Learning to develop settings could take several minilessons. You could study the kinds of details that help readers visualize where and when the story is taking place—how to show if the setting is inside or outside, how to use background details to show what room the character is in, describing whether it's day or night or a certain season. That would represent a chunk of minilessons.

Another secondary goal might focus on taking risks in your illustrations. You might spend just one minilesson on risk taking, but then during conferences, continue to support students to take risks by drawing things that are hard to draw. You'll likely do this more with some students than others, so this goal might need only one whole-class minilesson but multiple individual or small group conferences.

Another possible secondary goal is to increase stamina for writing. You might not teach students to write for longer periods during minilessons, but the by-product of a whole unit focused on supporting children's compositional thinking in their illustrations should be an increase in their stamina for writing.

### Number of Secondary Goals

There is no magic number of secondary goals, but we usually recommend four to eight. If we just have one or two then our teaching is probably not ambitious enough. On the other hand, if we have fifteen goals we'll spend all of our time on assessment and less time on teaching. We advocate four to eight goals because that number helps us focus our teaching and assessment without becoming a checklist of skills taught without regard for learning.

### Types of Secondary Goals

When projecting a unit of study we consider a broad range of secondary goals beyond those that just describe the qualities of good writing. We definitely include writing-quality goals, but we also want to look at the total picture of the child as a writer.

Much of our thinking about goals comes from Stephanie Parsons' books *First Grade Writers* and *Second Grade Writers*. In these books Stephanie helps teachers think about a range of goals that support each child's complete development as a writer. By having goals that focus on, for example, children's interaction with their peers to form a community of writers, Stephanie helps us remember that we need to consider the whole child when determining goals. In *First Grade Writers* and *Second Grade Writers* Stephanie focuses on four categories of goals: writing quality, writing conventions, writing habits, and community.

In a recent conversation with Stephanie as we prepared to write this chapter, she talked about her thinking regarding goals. Stephanie said, "Setting goals beyond or outside of what our state or local standards might require gives us a chance to voice what we value in our teaching. Of course we teach about qualities of writing and conventions, but we can also help children see that writing is a human endeavor, not just a task to be completed at school."

Like us, Stephanie is inspired by Carl Anderson's thinking about looking at writers through various lenses in order to see them in different ways. As Stephanie says, "Having different goals helps us look beyond spelling, for example, and see more clearly what a child is able to do to explore a personal interest, engage an audience, or tell a story well."

Stephanie also emphasized goals that are important for young writers. She said, "I think about the importance of goals that impact a writer's identity. For example, we might become frustrated by the fact that a child writes over and over about going to the park, but having goals related to a writer's identity changes how we look at this writer and how we can use a favorite topic to our advantage and teach them how to write about a meaningful topic in different ways."

Ultimately you will have to decide what goals are most important to you; the goals listed on our projection template are meant simply to be guides (see Appendix B). What you value will come through in your goals.

In addition to the four types of goals Stephanie describes, most of our units have a goal focused on revision. We also usually include editing goals among the conventions goals. The next sections look briefly at each type of secondary goal.

### Writing-Quality Goals

Teachers want their students to learn to produce high-quality writing. However, evaluating writing can be subjective. Fortunately, in addition to your own ideas, there is a base of literature from various authors that describes what exemplifies good writing.

There are several lists of qualities of good writing that we believe in. Many teachers are familiar with *6 + 1 Traits of Writing* (Culham 2003), which focuses on ideas, word choice, sentence fluency, voice, organization, and conventions. Katie Wood Ray focuses on four qualities in her book *In Pictures and In Words* (2010): ideas and content, precision and detail, wholeness of text, and tone. We also often use Carl Anderson's (2005) list of qualities: meaning, genre, structure, details, voice, and conventions.

Whichever list you (or your district) use, it can provide a framework for designing secondary goals that address the qualities of good writing. If your district doesn't use one of these lists, you can choose the resources that make the most sense to you. In most units of study you will design secondary goals that address at least a few of these qualities. Having a list of the qualities of good writing handy, along with state standards and district curricula, helps you think of possible goals, especially when you're stuck. Asking yourself questions like, "Is this a unit where I particularly want to focus on organization?" or "What kind of details do I want to focus on in this unit?" will help you write secondary goals. Here are two examples of secondary goals based on writing quality to spark your thinking:

- Students will organize their feature article in a way that makes it both logical and engaging for the reader.
- Students will show rather than tell character emotions and feelings.

### Writing-Habits Goals

Student dispositions are important in creating the conditions and mind-sets needed for students to write well. In addition to goals about writing quality, most units of study will have a goal focused on writing habits. Sometimes these are related to the particular unit of study, but often they are based on what students need at a particular time of year.

Writing-habits goals can be a bit nebulous and difficult to measure, yet that should not preclude them from being included in unit goals, because they encompass some of our most important long-term writing goals. For example, the goal "working with increased stamina" can be hard to put a number to, but we can assess it. We can describe what it looks like when students work with stamina. They produce a quantity of writing independently. While they talk to each other about their writing, they don't interrupt one another and get off task. They become lost in their writing and ask for a couple more minutes when writing time is over. However, these things will certainly be hard to address if we don't value writing habits enough to create a goal for them in the first place.

To design writing-habits goals we can look toward several sources—our own writing process, thoughts about process from authors we trust, and what our students are actually doing. When examining your process, ask yourself, "What habits do I have that help me write well?" It can also be helpful to read what authors say about their own writing processes. And perhaps most important, we can look at what our students are doing. What problems are your students encountering in the classroom? What habits and dispositions would make writing easier for them?

Here are a few examples of secondary goals based on writing habits to spark your thinking:

- In the kindergarten unit on launching writing workshop: "Students will engage in a process to find meaningful topics for books."

- In a second-grade illustration study: "Students will write with increased stamina and energy."

- In a fifth-grade study of the personal essay: "Students will show evidence of thinking about their writing projects outside of writing workshop."

### Writing-Community Goals

One of our big goals in a writing workshop at any age is for students to be comfortable sharing their writing and to respond constructively to each other's writing. For this to occur, teachers need to foster a sense of community in their writing workshops. Looking at a workshop as a community, rather than individual writers working on their own projects, requires attention on the part of the teacher. Communities need to be nurtured, so many units of study will have a goal focused on creating a community of writers. Of course, if we have such a goal, then we must spend some of our classroom time specifically teaching and modeling how to interact during writing workshop. If it's worth including as a goal, and we believe it is, then it's worth teaching time.

Here are two examples of secondary goals based on writing community:

- In a kindergarten illustration study focused on taking risk in illustrations, children's disposition toward taking risks is impacted by how their peers react to their illustrations, so we might design this classroom community goal: "Students will respond positively to each other's illustrations."

- A fifth-grade class studying historical fiction might have this goal: "Students show evidence of revising to take out less important details."

### Revision Goals

Several years ago Mary Alice started including a revision goal in each unit of study, and we've incorporated this practice into our process. Depending on the particular unit, Mary Alice would decide which type of revision to focus on: adding something in, taking something out, changing something, or moving something. Some units lend themselves to one type more than another. It seems that in most poetry units we focus on *changing*, especially revising for word choice. In many of our nonfiction units we focus on *taking out* less important details. In many of our story units we focus on *adding* details.

Of course, having a revision focus doesn't preclude us from teaching any type of revision when needed, whether in a minilesson or a conference. But having a focus helps keep revision in the forefront of our minds. We can't hold our students accountable for using revision strategies if we haven't taught them.

Here are a few examples of secondary goals based on revision:

- Students will revise for word choice by showing evidence of trying out and *changing* words in their poem.

- Students will show evidence of *adding* details, such as dialogue, to their realistic fiction story.

### Conventions and Editing Goals

We tend to include a conventions and/or editing goal in each unit. Spelling, punctuation, and grammar are crucial in writing. Of course, focusing *only* on conventions leaves out goals related to composition and process, which is why we suggest including a conventions goal as just one of several other types of goals. Some conventions and editing goals are specific to a particular unit of study. For example, in a unit on short fiction stories, it would make sense to write a goal focused on punctuating dialogue, since students will likely use dialogue in their stories. Other goals may not be tied directly to a unit, but rather are based on what students need at a particular time of year in a particular grade. A conventions goal in a first-grade class might be, "Students will use appropriate spacing between words." This goal could be a part of any unit, and would be included at a time of year when students were working on that skill.

# Determining the Difference Between Primary and Secondary Goals

There is not always a clear-cut difference between primary and secondary goals. Their importance depends on the particular emphasis of a unit. A primary goal in one classroom, grade level, or school could be a secondary goal in another. Factors such as district curriculum, grade level, and experience of the students will determine whether a goal is a primary goal, a secondary goal, or perhaps just a minilesson topic.

For example, imagine a unit on feature articles. Most teachers would include a goal about organization, such as, "Students will write an article that is organized into an introduction and logical sections." One group of teachers might determine that this is a secondary goal since they will spend a chunk of minilessons teaching students about the organization of feature articles. In another grade level in another school, organization might be a huge goal for students and might be the primary reason that a unit on feature articles was chosen to begin with. For those teachers, organization might be a primary goal.

Another group of teachers might say, "We already taught a lot about organization in an earlier nonfiction unit. In this unit we'll probably just spend one or two minilessons on organization." Figure 6.1 shows how one goal could fit as a primary goal, secondary goal, or minilesson topic depending on the grade level and focus for the unit.

**Figure 6.1** Factors Influencing Goal Type

| Goal: Students will write an article that is organized into an introduction and logical sections. | |
| --- | --- |
| **This goal would be a . . .** | **If . . .** |
| Primary Goal | • The teacher decides this is a particularly important skill for the unit. Or, <br> • The teacher plans to spend a significant amount of time on this goal. |
| Secondary Goal | • The teacher decides this skill is important but not the main focus for the unit. Or, <br> • The teacher decides she will spend three or four minilessons on organization. |
| Minilesson Topic | • The teacher feels her students organize their writing well and will just spend a day helping them think about organization for this type of writing. |

# Goals Evolve Throughout the Projecting Process

Once you've decided on primary and secondary goals, you're not necessarily finished with goal setting. At this point, you actually have *drafts* of goals rather than final goals, because as you continue to design the unit (projecting minilessons based on teaching possibilities you generated as well as on these goals), you may alter goals based on the teaching possibilities you decide to address. You might discover a goal that's missing. For example, while projecting a unit on poetry you might find that you plan to spend several days helping students find poetry topics. Even if this didn't initially occur to you as a goal, you might want to add, "Students will utilize strategies to independently generate topics for poems." It's important to make sure there is a match between your goals and what you are projecting you will teach.

You might also find that you eliminate or change a goal as you project miniles-son topics. But having these goals in mind now, even if they change a bit, provides direction as you project a sequence of minilessons for this unit.

# Using Primary and Secondary Goals as the Foundation for Assessment

Unit goals describe the most important things for students to learn and accomplish in a unit. Therefore, we certainly need to assess student progress toward these goals. In each unit we need a way of assessing each goal. Primary and secondary goals form the foundation of assessment.

There are a variety of ways we can assess student growth toward goals. For many goals, we can simply look at student writing at the end of the unit and determine whether or to what level a child has reached a goal. We want to be careful not to exclusively use student writing at the end of a unit as our sole assessment data point. We want to look beyond finished products. Here are some ways to consider using goals for assessment.

- **Assessing Goals During Conferences.** A significant source of assessment data is the notes we take during each writing conference. In our conferring notes we write down strengths that we see in each child as a writer. These notes are valuable for assessment because they show what we actually saw a child do on a given day. At the end of the unit we can go back through our conferring notes looking for evidence of what a child has accomplished. Of course, we're especially likely to write down strengths related to goals and assessment because we determined our goals up front. If we know we're going to assess something, we're more likely to notice it as we go through the unit.

- **Assessing Goals While Students Are Composing.** We can also collect data from student writing while it is in process, whether it's an unfinished piece of student writing in the primary grades or a draft in the intermediate grades. Looking at drafts of writing can provide us with valuable information regarding revision and editing. We need to see where students start in order to fully understand and appreciate where they end.

- **Assessing Goals During Whole-Group Teaching.** Finally, we can use anecdotal notes based on what we see during whole-group teaching as assessment data. For example, we can best find evidence for community of writers goals during whole-group teaching times because we need to gather data on student interactions.

## The Dilemma of Rubrics

We often receive questions about grading and the use of a rubric in assessment. We obviously care about assessing student writing because we care more about what students learn than what we have taught. Grading is putting a number to our assessment data. We can use rubrics, point systems, and checklists if necessary to provide a number, although we are more interested in the feedback a student receives that will help them grow than on a grade.

We have two concerns about using rubrics. One is that many of the rubrics we see, especially in the primary grades, place too much emphasis on spelling, grammar, and punctuation. We're not saying these areas shouldn't be assessed, but when 50 to 75 percent of the items on a rubric are related to conventions (as we frequently encounter), there is an imbalance. The other concern with rubrics is that they can lead teachers to be reductionist in their teaching (Wilson 2006). We often see teachers focusing only on what appears on the rubric, to the exclusion of teaching possibilities that would better meet a child's individual needs. Our vision for our students and assessment needs to be broader than most rubrics allow.

Setting goals provides you with a solid foundation for your unit. You will return to your goals as you expand into the exciting possibilities that await. In the next chapter you will see that we want teachers to think of more minilesson teaching points than time will permit. By having a broader bank of possible teaching points available, we can better meet a child where he is in his writing development and help nudge him forward.

# MARY ALICE'S REALISTIC FICTION UNIT:
## Determining Primary and Secondary Goals

### Determining Primary Goals

After studying their stack of realistic fiction, but before starting to project how the unit might unfold, Mary Alice and her colleagues discussed primary and secondary goals. They worked on primary goals first and kept several things in mind.

- They thought about their lifetime goals for students as writers.
- They thought about what they wanted students to accomplish by the end of the unit.
- Since realistic fiction is a genre-specific unit, they discussed the fundamental characteristics of realistic fiction. What key components of this genre did they want to see in their students' writing?
- They discussed their students' writing strengths and areas for growth in light of district goals and standards.

During their discussion they talked about how they wanted to make sure their students' energy and motivation for writing stayed high during this unit, knowing that energy for writing was important in learning to write well. They shared their thoughts about what makes realistic fiction realistic fiction, as well as anticipating some of the difficulties students would have as they tackled this type of writing for the first time. They talked about the wide range of student abilities and how they would need to be particularly comfortable with first graders' realistic fiction stories that look like they were made by first graders (which makes perfect sense—they *are* first graders). Finally, they knew that they would have to let some things go and not get wrapped up in trying to make their students write great "plots" and instead focus more on the qualities of good story writing.

With this thinking in mind, they settled on the primary goals shown in Figure 6.2.

**Figure 6.2** Mary Alice's Primary Goals

1. **Students will write make-believe stories that could really happen.**

2. **Students will utilize various crafting techniques and types of details.**

The first goal may sound like it simply restates the unit of study, and in a way, it does. Because this would be students' first time writing realistic fiction, and also their first genre study of the year, actually writing realistic fiction at all was a significant enough goal. They anticipated that some students might have difficulty writing within a specific genre for the first time that year, and others might be challenged by writing a fictional story as opposed to the true stories they had written in kindergarten.

They felt that the second goal spoke to their desire for students to not just write stories, but to write them well. They knew that students would notice, and teachers would point out, specific techniques that writers of realistic fiction stories utilize, so they wanted to see evidence of students trying these techniques and skills in their own writing. Notice that the goals are action-oriented and focused on things that students will *do*.

With two big goals in mind, they were ready to think about secondary goals.

## Determining Secondary Goals

Next Mary Alice and her colleagues discussed secondary goals. They examined the list of teaching possibilities generated while studying the mentor texts and kept an eye out for patterns and groups of skills. They also relied on their previous discussion about their students' development as writers at that point in the year and what they hoped their next areas of growth might be. Figure 6.3 shows their secondary goals.

**Figure 6.3** Mary Alice's Secondary Goals

1. Students will generate multiple sentences on most of their pages.

2. Quality of writing—organization: Students will write stories that have a beginning, a series of events, and an ending.

3. Writing habit—prewriting: Students will prewrite by discussing their characters and the problem and solution of their story with a partner before writing.

4. Community of writers: Students will become more effective at talking with their partners about their stories before they start writing.

5. Revision: Students will show evidence of revising by adding details into their writing.

6. Editing conventions: Students will use appropriate capitalization more consistently.

Here are Mary Alice's reasons for setting each of these secondary goals for her class.

*Goal 1*: Many of her students were writing just one or two sentences on a page. She wanted to help students increase the quantity of their writing.

*Goal 2*: She wanted her students to understand that stories have more middle than beginning or end. She used this language from the Common Core.

*Goals 3 and 4*: These goals are closely linked. Mary Alice wanted her students to become better at thinking about their stories in advance, and talking with a partner seemed a developmentally appropriate way to do that. But this meant they needed to be able not just to think about their stories in advance but also to practice the skill of talking with a partner about their books. Thinking about your story is a writing-habit goal that impacts quality. Talking with someone effectively is a community of writers goal.

*Goal 5*: Mary Alice set this revision goal because she anticipated that students would go back into their stories and add the types of details they were noticing in the texts they were studying. The other type of revision she considered was revising by changing, by focusing on word choice. While she certainly expected to address word choice in minilessons and conferences, she felt her bigger emphasis would be on adding details.

*Goal 6*: Mary Alice knew that she would need to teach how to capitalize proper names because students would be creating characters. It seemed a good time to think about capitalization in general.

Finally, Mary Alice decided to make her own realistic fiction picture book. She knew she would need to be able to show her students her own writing. This would enable her to model reading like a writer by showing how she was trying out the very techniques they were noticing in their stack. Going through the process herself would help Mary Alice better understand, and prepare for, the process her students would experience.

With their goals in hand they were ready to move on, remembering that these were draft goals because some of them might change once they started to project possible minilesson topics.

## PROJECTING A UNIT IN THE INTERMEDIATE GRADES

### Determining Primary Goals

The process for thinking about goals in the intermediate grades is very similar to the process Mary Alice and her colleagues went through. The content of the conversation will be different, given the increased experience level and sophistication of intermediate writers.

For fourth graders, simply writing realistic fiction isn't a significant enough goal; that would be implied. Figure 6.4 shows the primary goals from a group of fourth-grade teachers projecting a unit on realistic fiction.

The intermediate students in this class would be working on many of the techniques that Mary Alice's students would work on, but with a higher level of sophistication. Teachers' expectations are higher. For example, Mary Alice's students would certainly talk about character traits, but Mary Alice wasn't expecting her students to do it well enough to include it as a primary goal. Fourth-grade students' realistic fiction should show evidence that they are working on developing characters with clear traits.

### Determining Secondary Goals

Once again, the process for thinking about secondary goals is similar in the intermediate grades. Teachers discussed strengths and areas for growth in terms of the qualities of good writing and district goals and standards. The realistic fiction secondary goals for the fourth-grade team are listed in  Figure 6.5.

**Figure 6.4** Fourth-Grade Realistic Fiction Primary Goals

1. Students will develop characters with clear character traits.
2. Students will write realistic fiction stories with events that connect in a logical way.
3. Students will articulate which techniques they used to make their story and why.

**Figure 6.5** Fourth-Grade Realistic Fiction Secondary Goals

1.  Writing quality: Students will write with varied sentence length and complexity.

2.  Writing quality: Students will write descriptively to help the reader understand characters, setting, and actions in their stories.

3.  Revision: Students will revise for word choice and descriptive language.

4.  Writing quality—structure: Students' stories will show some type of change, either in the characters and/or in what happens in the story.

5.  Writing quality: Students will use dialogue effectively.

6.  Community of writers: Students will ask partners for feedback on a specific part xof their story.

## ✎ Try It Out

1.  Create a list of your lifetime goals for writers. You'll keep these lifetime goals in mind throughout the year as they stretch over every unit.

    1. _____

    2. _____

    3. _____

2.  After studying the stack you collected for this particular unit, determine one to three primary goals based on standards, district curricula, and your list of teaching possibilities. Write a draft of the goals and consider whether they are too broad or too specific.

    1. _____

    2. _____

    3. _____

3.  Next determine secondary goals. Usually you'll have four to eight. You don't necessarily need one goal for each category below, but to consider various types of goals try to come up with at least one for each type.

    **Writing Quality** _____

    **Writing Quality** _____

    **Writing Quality** _____

    **Writing Habits** _____

    **Community of Writers** _____

    **Revision** _____

    **Editing/Conventions** _____

4.  After brainstorming multiple different types of goals, decide which ones you want to include at this point and record them on your projection template (Appendix B), keeping in mind that your goals may change after you go through the process of projecting teaching possibilities for the unit.

# Projecting Minilessons and Anticipating Issues

Now that you've named the unit, studied the stack of mentor texts to pull out teaching possibilities, and determined primary and secondary goals, you know a lot about what you could teach. When you jot down teaching possibilities with colleagues while studying a stack, you generate many more ideas than you'll have time to teach. The challenge becomes narrowing down this list of teaching possibilities as you project minilessons, small groups, and conferences.

If you've ever packed for a camping trip, you understand the difficulty in narrowing down. When you're going camping, you know you'll need certain items, like food, clothing, and a tent. There are also things you'd like to take but don't think you'll have room for in your backpack: the extra guidebook, the extra pair of socks. And then there are items you may need, but you're not sure. Should you take the rain poncho even though the forecast is clear? Should you take the extra canteen, anticipating that you may not have access to drinkable water? Do you take the heavy-duty hiking boots or more comfortable gym shoes, knowing that you can't take both? Ultimately you have to make some hard decisions because you have only so much room in your pack. You have to decide what will make the cut and what you will leave behind.

This same concept holds true for projecting your unit. Let's start by thinking about the basic building block of the writing workshop—minilessons. There will be some minilesson topics you know you will need, some you won't have room for, and others you aren't sure about including. Unlike packing for a trip, however, you can swap a minilesson that didn't make the cut for one that did at any point in a unit.

# Projecting Minilesson Topics

Now that you have primary and secondary goals, you're ready to return to the list of teaching possibilities that you created while studying the stack of mentor texts. You'll use this list to project a possible sequence of lessons that give you an idea of how this unit could unfold (knowing that it won't unfold exactly as you expect). It is important to note that at this point you're simply determining *topics* for minilessons. You're not creating lesson plans.

Here is our sequence of steps for projecting minilesson topics, each discussed in greater depth below.

1. Determine how long the unit will last.

2. Consider how many days you might need for immersion.

3. List possible minilesson topics in the Possible Minilesson Topics section of the projection template (see Appendix B), based on the list of teaching possibilities you generated as you studied your stack, what you've discovered about the process of creating this type of writing, your knowledge of child development, and what you envision students will need to know to create this type of writing.

4. Consider how many days you might need to get ready for the writing celebration.

5. Correlate minilesson topics with primary and secondary goals.

6. Narrow down minilesson topics.

7. Group like minilesson topics together.

8. Put minilessons in order.

## TIPS FOR MORE EFFICIENT MINILESSON TOPIC PROJECTION

Here's a tip for an easier way to fill out your projection of minilessons. First determine approximately how many immersion days you will need for this unit and write them in. Then skip ahead and determine how many days it will take to get ready for the celebration, and write those days in, along with the celebration day. Then fill in all of the days that come in between. The advantage of this method is that it gives you an idea right away of how many days you have to teach the bulk of the unit.

## Determine How Long the Unit Will Last

The first step is to determine how long the unit of study will last, since that will determine how many minilessons can be included. Most units will last three to six weeks. It's difficult to study a unit in depth in less than three weeks. If you include a

## PLANNING MINILESSONS

Before we teach a minilesson we of course thoroughly plan it. That type of planning is beyond the scope of this book. For more information on planning minilessons, see our list of unit planning resources in Appendix A. We find these questions helpful to keep in mind as we plan minilessons:

- What is the one clear goal for this minilesson?

- Will we use a published mentor text, our own writing, student writing, or a combination of these during the lesson?

- How will we activate students' prior knowledge?

- Will students practice the skill or technique taught before going off to write, and if so, how?

- Will the lesson be inquiry based or more teacher directed? Who will do the noticing?

This just scratches the surface of planning minilessons. At this point in the projection process we are concerned with *what* we will teach, not *how* we will teach it. We'll determine how we will teach a minilesson topic closer to the actual day we will teach it.

couple of days of immersion, a couple of days getting ready for the celebration, and then a day for the actual celebration, one week is gone already, which would only leave two more weeks in a three-week unit. On the flip side, a unit that goes for eight or nine weeks becomes tiring for both teachers and students, and students lose energy for the study.

Some units tend to last longer than others. In the primary grades, units such as Where Writers Get Ideas or Punctuation Study might be on the shorter end, while Literary Nonfiction or Realistic Fiction might take longer. Where Writers Get Ideas is generally a shorter unit with a narrower focus—we're not studying specific crafting techniques. In the intermediate grades, a study of reviews would tend to be on the shorter end of the spectrum, while a personal essay unit might take longer since personal essays are more complex and a more difficult type of writing than reviews.

Of course you also have to take into account student energy. Students might have a lot of energy for writing reviews and be able to write numerous reviews over a longer period of time. But they might have less energy for writing essays. While student energy isn't the only determining factor, it is one to consider.

Finally, you need to look at any district requirements before deciding how long a unit will be. If your district requires students to produce a certain number of different types of writing in a grading period, or for certain types of writing to be done at a certain time of year, the length of your units might have to be adjusted accordingly. Your primary goals can help you make these decisions.

### Consider How Many Days You Might Need for Immersion

There are many different ways to handle the immersion phase of a unit of study. You will decide what makes the most sense as you begin your unit. It is important to block out time for immersion, however you decide to do it.

### Immersion in Genre Studies

The length of the immersion phase will be determined in part by whether or not students have studied this particular genre before. If students are new to the genre, immersion will take a bit longer, perhaps three or four days. Fifth graders writing their first essay will need more days of reading essays than fifth graders writing poetry (which they have studied several times in previous years). First graders studying literary nonfiction will need more immersion than first graders studying illustration, since they've already been illustrating and can start making books quickly.

In the primary grades, the first several days of a unit are spent reading the new genre and becoming familiar with how that genre is different from other types of writing students know. In intermediate classrooms, teachers generally spend the first couple of days reading aloud examples of the new genre and then the class discusses what they notice. On subsequent days the students read examples of the new genre independently, making notes about what they notice.

### Immersion in Non-Genre-Specific Studies

The same things could happen in a non-genre-specific study, like an illustration or punctuation study in the primary grades. In an illustration study, the teacher might read a book that would help introduce the unit, like the first story of Laura Vaccaro Seeger's *Dog and Bear: Two Friends, Three Stories*, to show what she means by illustration techniques. In a punctuation study, she might read *Yo! Yes?* by Chris Raschka to highlight the ways that punctuation changes how writing sounds. Then she might give partners a picture book and some sticky notes and have them put the notes on examples of illustration techniques or interesting punctuation. In both of these units, the students could start making picture books right from the beginning, but teachers generally spend a couple of days immersing students in texts that illustrate the focus of the study.

Immersion is possible in some process studies as well. Let's take the unit Where Writers Find Ideas, in either the primary or intermediate grades, as an example. Students could certainly start writing projects right away in this unit. But we could also spend the first day or two helping students understand that the main goal for this new unit is for them to independently generate meaningful ideas. We could share our own process and explain that our own energy for writing increases when we have a topic that is especially meaningful. On the first day we might start a list of meaningful topics and then look at several texts for evidence of where the author got the idea for text. While we could start writing on those first couple of days, we wouldn't have to.

## List Possible Minilesson Topics

After filling in the immersion days on the projection template, we start listing the minilesson topics. At this point we don't want to get bogged down in determining the perfect lesson from day to day, so rather than trying to build the projection sequentially, we just list all of the minilesson topics we might want to teach in this unit. At this point we don't limit our list to the number of lessons we'll actually teach. There are two big reasons why it's better to project more minilesson topics than there are available days.

- At any point in the unit we might decide to take one of the lesson topics that we didn't have time for and put it back in the projected sequence of lessons.

- When conferring with students, we might decide to teach a topic that we had considered but then cut from our minilesson list.

By considering everything we might teach, we build a bank of possible teaching points for writing conferences that we might need at any time. We expand, rather than narrow, the range of what we might teach and therefore can make our instruction more powerful for individual students.

We also want to guard against presenting a new topic each day of a unit. Topic-a-day teaching often doesn't provide students with the depth of understanding to actually try a technique or skill in their writing. One day might be enough to help students notice a technique, like how authors use repetition in a story, but it may take more experience with this technique for them to actually *use* repetition in their writing. Some topics can be covered in a day and others will take longer to explore. The temptation is to try to fit in too many topics, which can lead to superficial teaching. In general we advocate for fewer topics taught in greater depth. The more minilesson topics we project, the more we have to choose from as we teach the unit, and the more responsive we can be to our students' needs.

### Consider How Many Days You Might Need to Get Ready for the Writing Celebration

When listing minilesson topics we always reserve the final day of the unit for a celebration. This is the day we make our writing public by sharing it with others. In her book *Hidden Gems*, Katherine Bomer makes an excellent case for the importance of writing celebrations (2010). We've included a brief list of a few possible types of celebrations in Appendix F. But for the purpose of unit projection, simply write in "Celebration" on the last day of your unit; you will think more about *how* you'll celebrate later.

It's also important to set aside days for students to get their writing ready to share. We generally allow two to four getting-ready days. These typically include a day or two of final revision (students' last chance to add, delete, change, or move anything in their writing) and a day or two of final editing. During this time, students do everything they need to do to get their writing ready to share. In the primary grades that might mean adding a fancy cover or an author's note. In the intermediate grades students might make their final decision about the font for their title before printing their writing from the computer.

### Correlate Minilesson Topics with Primary and Secondary Goals

When you think you have projected all of the minilessons, look back at your primary and secondary goals and see if there are minilessons connected to each goal. Frequently teachers look back at secondary goals in particular and find a goal or two with no whole-group teaching attached to it.

There are three things you can do when this happens.

- Add minilesson topics related to this goal. In our experience, this is what happens most frequently.

- Remove the goal. If you just spent time projecting minilessons for this unit and it never crossed your mind to include lessons related to this goal, then perhaps it didn't need to be a goal to begin with.

- Leave it as is. In our experience this happens least frequently. Very occasionally, you'll have written a goal that has no associated minilessons. For example, a goal for a unit early in the year may be for students to develop greater stamina for writing. Increased stamina could be a by-product of multiple minilessons on helping students choose meaningful topics. Another possibility is to address this goal during conferences and share time rather than in a minilesson.

### Narrow Down Minilesson Topics

After listing all of the possible minilesson topics, the next step is to narrow the list to fit the number of teaching days you have left after factoring in immersion days, getting-ready days, and the celebration day. There are several ways to think about which days to remove from your initial list of projected minilesson topics.

You might combine some topics into a single day's teaching. Of course, you'll want to make sure you're not trying to pack too much into one lesson, but in some cases it makes sense to cover related topics on one day—for example, in a primary illustration study you may have planned to focus one day on how to zoom in on an illustration to show that an object is close and another day on how to zoom out to show that an object is far away. If you think your students will grasp this concept quickly, you might decide to teach these related concepts on the same day. In an intermediate unit on How-to Articles you may have thought about spending one day on giving your reader warnings about what could go wrong, and another day on telling your reader what to actually do if something goes wrong. Remember, though, in general, consider having fewer topics with more depth rather than more topics with less depth.

Here are some additional suggestions for creating a focused list of minilesson topics:

- Reduce the number of days on one topic. Let's say you had projected that you would spend three days teaching how to skillfully use bits of dialogue. You might decide that you can do this in two days.

- Take out lessons that don't feel necessary. You can keep these topics in mind for conferring and small-group work.

Remember, you're not really eliminating the lessons that don't make the cut. Instead you'll place them in the Other Teaching Possibilities section of the planning template. At any point during the unit, you might swap a lesson that made the cut for one that didn't based on the needs of your students. Also, putting them in this "parking lot" rather than simply deleting them will help you remember that you might need this topic at any point during a writing conference.

### Group Similar Minilesson Topics Together

Once you've narrowed your projection down to the appropriate number of days, the next step is to group lessons together. You probably naturally did this to some extent as you projected the unit. You may have already grouped all of your lessons on developing a setting or developing essay topics. Take a moment to go back over your projection and see if there are any lessons that need to be taught sequentially. Most lessons fall into clear categories: finding topics, planning and organization, process lessons, craft lessons, detail lessons, revision lessons, and so forth. Keeping these categories in mind can help you decide how to group your minilessons. It can be helpful to keep track of the category each teaching possibility falls into when writing them on the projection sheet, like this:

Detail: Using dialogue

Detail: Showing emotions and feelings

Detail: Showing internal thinking

### Put Minilessons in Order

The last step is to move lessons into the most logical order. Lessons on finding writing topics may need to go earlier in the unit, a lesson on a particular crafting technique may need to be moved later, a conventions lesson might need to be bumped up a few days, and so on. Again, the order is just your best guess of what makes the most sense since the order will likely change after the unit starts.

There are several factors to consider when thinking about sequencing minilessons:

- Determine which lessons students need right away. Decide which lessons will launch students into working independently and place them first.

- If the unit is a genre study, determine which lessons (in addition to the immersion days) will help students understand the key characteristics of this genre.

- Place craft lessons toward the middle of the unit. Students can start drafting without knowing every craft technique they might use since they will be able to add them as they revise.

- Think about existing prerequisite relationships between lessons. Do students need to learn a technique or skill in one lesson so that they can build on it in the next? For example, students might need a lesson on generating a list of possible story ideas before they can try one idea by writing about it in their notebook. Many lessons *don't* have a prerequisite relationship. You don't need to know how to use dialogue in a story before you learn how to show character emotions, for example. Consider what prerequisite relationships do exist in your teaching possibilities so that you can order minilessons accordingly.

## INSIGHTS FROM A TEACHER

After teaching fourth grade for ten years, I recently moved to first grade. Changing grades can be daunting. As the new school year began, I remember feeling like a first-year teacher all over again. Creating a new curriculum is tough work, but it needed to be done. Or did it? Next to me sat a thick stack of writing units, already written for me. I could just follow these units and my work would be done. But as I read over the first prewritten unit of study, the goals just didn't seem to mesh with what I was already learning about what my children needed. As I observed my class the first couple of days of school in writing workshop, I found myself quickly coming up with goals and minilessons based on my day-to-day experiences with them. I realized that we needed to work on intentionally planning our books and thinking carefully about composing pages. I realized that my children needed to discover the benefits of partner talk and how collaborating within a community of writers would help them further grow their ideas. I needed to learn about who my children were as writers, and craft lessons to meet their needs. Sure, I would pull from experts to help me along the way, but in the end, just studying my children each day would be the biggest unit of study I would need.

*—Laurie Smilack, first grade teacher, Atlanta*

# Writing Conferences

One of the questions we frequently hear from teachers is, "How do you know what to teach during a conference?" The process you've gone through will help you confer with writers because the first step in deciding what to teach is knowing what you *could* teach. And one of the big advantages of projecting units is that you have a large bank of possible teaching points for writing conferences. In a writing conference, teachers usually consider several possible teaching points, rather than just jumping to the first thing they see. But if you don't have multiple possibilities from which to choose, all you can teach is the first thing you think of, which may not be what will help students the most. It can be helpful to bring your list of teaching possibilities along with you as you confer. The more teaching possibilities you have to choose from, the more you are able to meet each student's needs during a conference.

# Anticipated Issues

On the projection template, you'll notice a section called Anticipated Issues. This is a place where you can keep track of issues that you anticipate may arise during the unit. You might:

- Think about the things that challenged your students the last time you taught this unit. What aspects of this unit seemed to be the easiest and the most difficult for previous students?

- Consider issues that are typical for students at your grade level. What do most second or fourth graders do? What is developmentally appropriate for the students you work with?

- Consider areas where you will need more data about students before you can make an informed decision. As you're projecting, you might come up with topics that you think you *might* need to teach, but you're not sure. Put these topics in the Anticipated Issues section.

- Consider how this year's class is different from last year's class. What different challenges might this group face in this unit? Even if you have taught a unit before, you are teaching to a new group of students each year and you will base the pacing and order of your teaching points as the unit progresses on the students you have in front of you.

- Consider the challenges you yourself would face if you were going to produce writing in this unit. Thinking about this might be particularly helpful if you've never taught this unit before.

- Envision possible small-group conferences. Jot a list of topics that you don't imagine you'll need to cover as a whole-class minilesson, but might need to teach in a small-group writing conference. For example, you might project that you'll spend two days helping your kindergartners find writing topics, but that four students will need additional support finding topics and might need a few small-group conferences. (Of course, you won't know for sure until the unit starts.)

The Anticipated Issues section is also where you might capture thoughts related to the needs of students who might benefit from extra support as well as those who benefit from extra enrichment. The students in most elementary classes represent a wide range of academic development. Because minilessons take place as whole-group instruction, they focus on what most students need. If only a few students need a topic, it's not effective to teach it to the whole class. That doesn't mean we don't need to thoughtfully prepare to meet each student's needs. The challenge of any type of whole-group teaching, including minilessons, is that some of our students may not be ready for that day's topic, while other students may have already mastered it. Expecting that we will have a wide range of students, we have to consider the supports and strategies we will use for individual students.

For example, in a typical third-grade class we expect to have several students for whom the act of transcription (getting words on the page) is very difficult—even though they have great ideas, they appear to be reluctant writers. When projecting a unit, you might consider (and record in the Anticipated Issues section) strategies that will help this group of students to plan their ideas in advance orally and then graphically so they can think through their whole text before writing.

## STUDYING OTHER PEOPLE'S UNITS

After you've projected your minilessons, you might look at units created by other teachers. Looking at someone else's unit might help you find something that you missed and want to add. More likely, it will confirm what you created. The key is that your knowledge of what to teach in this unit will be significantly deeper after going through the process of determining what to teach. Moreover, your overall understanding of writing will strengthen with each subsequent unit you project.

In that same third-grade class, there will likely be several students who try every technique we barely even mention. These students sometimes leave us scratching our head, trying to figure out what to teach or, even worse, tempting us to simply say, "Great job. Keep going." Of course, these students deserve to be taught something as well. When projecting the unit you will want to think of skills that might normally be taught to more experienced writers—ones that will stretch these students' thinking. A good place to look for these topics is in the Other Teaching Possibilities section of your template, where you likely placed some topics or techniques that you noticed when studying your stack, but decided wouldn't fit for most of your students.

## What's Next?

You're ready to begin your unit with your students! You've studied mentor texts with colleagues and pulled out teaching possibilities, determined goals, projected mini-lesson topics, and anticipated issues that might arise for your students. Now all of the benefits of envisioning how this unit could unfold will pay off as you embark on it with your students. Of course, even as prepared as you are, you'll still likely modify your unit as it progresses based on your observations of your writers and their writing. In the next chapter we will show how reflecting on your unit along the way will help you stay focused on, and responsive to, the needs of your students.

## PROJECTING A UNIT OF STUDY: Mary Alice's Realistic Fiction Unit

### Projecting a Possible Sequence of Minilessons

After deciding on a unit, gathering a stack of texts to study, and determining goals, Mary Alice and her colleagues started to project a possible sequence of minilessons. They knew that their sequence would quickly change once they started the unit, but they also knew that their day-to-day decision making would be much more powerful if they had a range of possibilities in mind.

Projecting the actual minilessons wasn't too difficult and didn't take long because of all of the thinking they had already done. If they had started the projection process by attempting to plan minilessons, they probably would have felt overwhelmed. But for Mary Alice and her colleagues, projecting minilessons was rather enjoyable because of everything they had done leading up to it:

- They had thoughtfully considered which unit would meet their students' needs at this point in the year. They knew this study was actually a good match, rather than just coming next in the calendar.

- They had carefully selected their stack of mentor texts. They felt their stack defined what they wanted students to do and would give them a vision for what they could make.

- They had spent a significant amount of time studying their stack. They knew the longer they studied their chosen texts, the more they would understand about realistic fiction and the possibilities for their students.

- They had also studied the process of what authors do when writing realistic fiction, even making their own books to better understand what their students would experience.

If they hadn't invested time in the earlier parts of the process, projecting possible minilesson topics would likely have been time consuming and frustrating. This step would also have taken longer if they had been creating plans for entire minilessons rather than just focusing on minilesson topics. Of course, as they discussed minilesson topics someone would occasionally mention an effective minilesson plan they had used before and wanted to use again. Or, sometimes they would briefly discuss ideas for teaching a specific skill. But for the most part, they kept their thinking focused on the unit as a whole rather than ideas for individual lessons. They knew they would have plenty of opportunities later to share ideas for the teaching that would occur each day.

**Figure 7.1** Mary Alice's Projection Template: List of Minilessons Dedicated to Immersion

**Projection of Possible Minilesson Topics**

1. Immersion
2. Immersion
3. Immersion: start writing

Mary Alice and her colleagues looked at the calendar and decided they would spend four to five weeks on this unit. They decided to shoot for a four-week unit, which would allow them a little cushion in case they needed a few extra days (which typically happens).

First, they started by thinking about the immersion part of the unit. They knew that they would need to spend several days just reading and talking about realistic fiction. Their students weren't totally unfamiliar with realistic fiction since they had been reading it in reading workshop. But Mary Alice and her colleagues did feel it might be difficult for students to make the transition to writing in this genre, so they knew they would need some immersion days. Mary Alice decided on three days of immersion for her class, knowing that in reality students might need one day more or less. She added to her projection template as shown in Figure 7.1.

Next, Mary Alice wrote in "Celebration" on day twenty (she was contemplating sharing their books with a preschool class in the school). Since she knew there would be a celebration day, she knew she'd have to project a few days for students to select a book they wanted to share and to get ready for the celebration.

Then Mary Alice and her colleagues pulled out the list of teaching possibilities they'd created while studying their stack. They started filling in topics for minilessons. They didn't worry too much about the order or which ones should go together, because they knew they would do some rearranging at the end. They also didn't spend time now debating which ones would be the most important to teach.

In Figure 7.2 you can see what Mary Alice's projection sheet looked like after they listed everything they might teach. Since this a book about projecting units, not about realistic fiction, we don't give an explanation for every item, but we do want to point out a few important things.

**Figure 7.2** Mary Alice's Projection Template: Initial List of Minilesson Topics

## Projection of Possible Minilesson Topics

1. Immersion
2. Immersion
3. Immersion: start writing
4. Planning/thinking ahead: character–external description
5. Planning/thinking ahead: character–internal description
6. Planning/thinking ahead: problem–keeping it real
7. Planning/thinking ahead: solution–keeping it real
8. Organizing: beginning
9. Organizing: end
10. Writing in third person
11. Audience/purpose: celebration
12. Setting: deciding and describing
13. Interesting openings and endings
14. Dialogue
15. Internal dialogue
16. Blow-by-blow details
17. Character feelings
18. Character internal thinking
19. Show not tell
20. Celebration
21. Tell rather than show
22. Passage of time
23. Capitalization: names
24. Setting: illustrations
25. Setting: words
26. Planning/thinking ahead: setting
27. Adding details: specific
28. Adding details: illustrations–character feelings
29. Rereading: edit punctuation
30. Rereading: edit capitalization
31. Prepare for celebration: select text–read to partner–be sure you can read
32. Prepare for celebration: expression and fluency

- You'll notice they have thirty-two days. They didn't stop when they got to twenty. Before they started they knew that they'd end up with more to teach than they'd have time for, but they didn't want to eliminate any possibilities.

- Even though they didn't list the lesson topics from the start sequentially, there were some topics that they knew they would want to address early on (characters, problems/solutions, planning), so they went ahead and put them early-ish in the unit (computers make this easy).

- They knew that during the immersion phase they wanted students to have a good understanding of what realistic fiction is and its purpose.

- You'll see several days on illustration. Mary Alice and her colleagues wanted to connect back to an illustration study from earlier in the year to help their students think about the parallels in their thinking when they compose with pictures and words.

After examining all of their possibilities, they decided to look at a unit created by another first-grade teacher to see if there were any topics they had missed. In comparing the units they noted numerous similarities and a few differences. The other unit didn't have any days on illustration. They decided that they certainly wanted to keep their illustration lessons. They also noticed that the other teacher had spent more time helping students create settings. Mary Alice and her colleagues discussed whether to add more days of focus on setting. They decided that since they would do some of that work in their illustration days, they were probably okay, but decided to add "may need more days on setting" in the Anticipated Issues section as a reminder.

Feeling good about the possibilities before them, Mary Alice and her colleagues started deciding which minilesson topics to move to the Other Teaching Possibilities section. Even though they wanted to teach them all, they had only so many days, so they prioritized which topics were most important. As they narrowed down their teaching, they also considered which topics should be grouped together. Then they looked at the topics once more and rearranged the order based on which topics should be taught before others. This was the point when the teachers' individual projection templates started to vary. Mary Alice thought her students might need more of one topic while a colleague felt her students would need less. Sometimes they changed the order of projected topics, based on the needs of their students. These were minor differences in terms of the whole unit, but significant for those particular students. In general, their units were similar but not identical, which makes sense because they had studied the same stack and created the unit together, yet kept in mind their own groups of students.

Figure 7.3 show's Mary Alice's template at this stage, the result of her prioritizing, grouping, and rearranging. You'll see that some of her topics are related to

**Figure 7.3** Mary Alice's Projection Template: Possible Minilesson Topics and Other Teaching Possibilities

**Projection of Possible Minilesson Topics**

1. Immersion: teacher noticings
2. Immersion: student noticings
3. Immersion: student noticings
4. Audience/purpose: celebration
5. Planning/thinking ahead: character–external and internal description
6. Planning/thinking ahead: problem and solution–keeping it real
7. Planning/thinking ahead: setting
8. Organizing: beginning, middle, end
9. Writing in third person
10. Illustrations: setting
11. Illustrations: character feelings
12. Dialogue
13. Character feelings: show not tell (what's in illustrations should also be in words)
14. Character feelings: internal thinking
15. Add details: blow by blow
16. Add detail: be specific
17. Capitalization (names)
18. Prepare for celebration: rereading and revising–more specific details
19. Prepare for celebration: read to partner–fluency and expression
20. Celebration

**Other Teaching Possibilities**

1. Passage of time
2. Telling character emotions
3. Interesting openings and endings

realistic fiction (creating characters), many are related to writing any type of story (dialogue), and others are needed in any type of writing (strategies for planning your writing).

Throughout the process of projecting her unit, Mary Alice had been thinking of issues that might arise, areas where students might have difficulty, and specific students who might need additional differentiated support. She added these items to the Anticipated Issue section so she would be reminded of them throughout the unit (Figure 7.4).

At this point, with her projection template in hand, Mary Alice was ready to begin the unit and start studying the stack of mentor texts with her students. She was eagerly anticipating discovering what they would notice and how they would respond to this exciting new genre.

**Figure 7.4** Mary Alice's Projection Template: Anticipated Issues

**Anticipated Issues**

1. Possible small-group conference–may have a small group of students who have a harder time transitioning from writing list books to writing stories.

2. May need to add another minilesson on creating settings.

3. Will need to remember to be very comfortable with their approximated plots, and focus more on the qualities of good writing.

4. Will have some students who may benefit from small-group conferences on showing rather than telling character emotions.

# PROJECTING A POSSIBLE SEQUENCE OF MINILESSONS IN THE INTERMEDIATE GRADES

The process for projecting, narrowing, regrouping, and sequencing topics is very similar in the intermediate grades. Intermediate teachers will also spend time thinking about goals and studying a stack of mentor texts before starting to project minilessons. Figure 7.5 shows the template sections Anticipated Issues, Projection of Possible Minilesson Topics, and Other Teaching Possibilities for a fourth-grade class. You'll notice that many of the broad topics are very similar, but the complexity and sophistication of what students will create is different from Mary Alice's first graders. Some differences are worth noting:

- This teacher decided to build her stack with short stories from children's magazines. For part of the immersion phase, she wanted students to read these stacks on their own to see what they could notice (something most of Mary Alice's first graders wouldn't have been able to do with their picture books). To do this, the fourth-grade teacher switched her writing partnerships, which usually paired good talking partners, to partnerships with varied reading levels to ensure that all students could read a story from the stack.

- In fourth grade, students were using a writer's notebook, so much of the early work in this unit was done in their notebooks. They also used notebook entries from throughout the year to search for seed ideas for their stories. For their drafts they used individual pieces of paper, since significant revisions would be easier on separate sheets than in a notebook.

- While Mary Alice's students made numerous books throughout the unit, this fourth-grade teacher was anticipating that most students would write one realistic fiction story, and a few might write more than one.

Again, while the teaching content and level of expectations were very different from those for Mary Alice's class, the process of projecting the unit was exactly the same.

**Figure 7.5** Projection Template: Fourth-Grade Possible Minilesson Topics, Teaching Possibilities, and Anticipated Issues

### Anticipated Issues

1. Students may overuse dialogue—may need additional minilessons or small-group conferences.
2. A few students may struggle to find a realistic problem and solution.

### Projection of Possible Minilesson Topics

1. Immersion: reading together
2. Immersion: reading independently—generate and share noticings
3. Using your notebook to find topics
4. Developing problems and solutions
5. Using a graphic organizer to plan my problem and solution
6. Characteristics of characters—developing character in writer's notebook
7. Choosing and describing a setting
8. Planning out my scenes (notebook)
9. Writing in scenes
10. Stretching out scenes
11. Dialogue: just bits
12. Dialogue: conventions, quotations, or new paragraph
13. Word choice: interesting adjectives
14. Emotions: actions that show emotions
15. Emotions: dialogue that shows emotions
16. Plot: conflict resolution, writing better endings
17. Recognizing and practicing leads
18. Revising for word choice
19. Editing for punctuation in dialogue
20. Celebration

### Other Teaching Possibilities

1. Word choice—options to said
2. Show character traits
3. Transitioning between scenes
4. Emotions and feelings: descriptive words
5. Choosing setting
6. Immersion: What makes realistic fiction realistic fiction, different from fantasy

**Try It Out**

Keep in mind that everything you include in the projected minilessons section can change once the unit starts. See Appendix B or go to www.heinemann.com/products/ E04192.aspx for a blank projection template.

1. In the Projection of Possible Minilesson Topics section write in how many days you think your students will need for immersion, considering how long you think it will take for them to get a feel for this genre or for the focus of this unit.

2. Next, write in "Celebration Day" for the last day of the unit.

3. Write in how many "getting ready" days you think students will need to get their writing ready to share.

4. Next, write down your remaining potential minilesson topics, based on the teaching possibilities you collected as you studied the stack of texts. Have your list of primary and secondary goals on hand to make sure you address them. Remember that you will likely have more potential mini-lessons than you will be able to teach.

5. Once you've recorded potential minilesson topics, narrow the possibilities to the number of days you have for the unit. You might combine some days, reduce the number of days on a topic, or take out some topics.

6. Place any topics that were removed in the Other Teaching Possibilities section of the template. You might use these in conferences or add them back as minilessons if needed.

7. Consider which minilesson topics should be grouped together.

8. Decide which minilesson topics should come early in the unit, in the middle, and toward the end. Make any needed changes to the order of the projected topics.

9. Record any issues that you envision arising in the Anticipated Issues section, keeping in mind groups of students who may struggle with this work as well as students who may benefit from enrichment.

# Responding and Reflecting During and After a Unit of Study

We believe that reflection is an invaluable part of teaching. We reflect throughout the course of the unit and make adjustments as we go in order to tailor our teaching to the needs of our students, and we reflect at the end of the unit as well. We see reflection as a crucial part of the projecting process, since reflection is actually the first step in projecting a unit the following year.

There are two main times you'll write in the reflections sections of the projection template—during the unit and after it. Reflections we make during the unit help us make the daily adjustments that keep our teaching truly responsive. Post-unit reflection encourages us to think about the unit's big picture, scope, and sequence. Both are important elements of projecting a unit of study that is truly based on students' needs.

## Making Responsive Changes Throughout the Unit

Once the unit is under way, you'll make changes at any point to ensure that you are meeting the needs of your students. You might take a lesson out, add one in, move a lesson earlier or later in the unit, stretch a lesson over two days, and so forth. When you projected the unit, you planned for these possibilities. In Chapter 1 we shared the following reasons that you might make adjustments during a unit.

- Students need more time to grasp a concept.
- Students are engaged with a topic and need more time.
- Students already know the skill you planned to introduce.
- Students want to try a skill you had not anticipated.
- Students need a skill or concept earlier than you had initially planned.
- Only a few students need help with a certain skill.

As you watch your students you'll notice when they grasp a concept easily or need more time. Listening carefully to student questions will lead you to rearrange upcoming lessons to address a common question that has arisen. Students might display an unanticipated interest in a technique they've noticed that you had considered teaching but not included in your projection, so you decide to reinsert it as a lesson. Looking at your students' writing, listening carefully to their questions, and being responsive to their "noticings" and interests will help you know when to make adjustments to your projected minilessons.

The following sections describe some of the many sources you can use to help you decide when to make adjustments during a unit.

### Preassessment Writing

Some teachers ask students to do a brief on-demand writing sample at the beginning of a new unit to assess what students already know about the kind of writing they will be doing. Teachers can then alter the subsequent minilessons if necessary. The writing sample can also provide information about individual students' strengths and areas for improvement. In deciding whether to ask their students to do some type of preassessment writing, teachers should consider the age of the students and whether this type of writing is new to the students.

### Student Responses and Questions During Minilessons and Conferences

As you interact with students during minilessons and conferences, you get a feel for student understanding. Student body language is often a great indicator of when a student is on track with your teaching. Student questions provide insight into what a child is understanding (or not understanding) during a minilesson or conference. Asking students to explain what you just taught will tell you how they are processing your teaching. Then back up your hunches ("I could just tell they weren't getting it") by analyzing what students actually do in their writing and looking for evidence of learning during conferences.

### Conferring Notes

Conferring notes provide a valuable source of information for needed adjustments in a unit. Many teachers record student strengths, what was taught in the conference, and next steps for the student in their conferring notes. With this valuable data teachers can more easily synthesize what is going well in the unit with needed adjustments by periodically analyzing their conferring notes. For example, a kindergarten teacher reviewing her conferring notes might realize that she has been having numerous conferences about staying on topic. She might decide to add a minilesson on this important skill. Or, a fifth-grade teacher might notice that her students are particularly good at making interesting word choices and so decide to teach fewer minilessons in this area than she originally projected.

### Student Writing Throughout the Unit

Throughout the unit you will want to survey student writing across the class. For example, early in a unit you might ask your students to leave their writing out before going to lunch, or you might take all students' writing home at the end of the day. You can then look at the writing across the class to get a feel for what students are doing well as well as common areas for improvement. There are several times during a unit when you might collect and survey student writing.

- **Early in a unit:** A first-grade teacher might look at children's writing early in an all-about/nonfiction unit to see if her students have made the transition from writing stories to informational texts.

- **Mid unit:** A fourth-grade teacher might collect drafts of her students' realistic fiction writing to see if students are including the types of details they have been studying in class.

- **Near the end of the unit:** A third-grade teacher might collect all of her students' writing a few days before the writing celebration to help her decide where to focus her final minilessons on revision.

Here's one example of how teachers make decisions to modify a unit once it is under way. Recently Matt worked with a team of second-grade teachers to project a unit of study on poetry. After studying a stack of poems they decided on primary and secondary goals and projected a possible sequence of minilesson topics. As they narrowed down their list of topics they discussed how many days they might spend on line breaks in poetry. At first they planned to spend three days on line breaks, but as they prioritized the most important things to teach they decided to include only one day on line breaks. They decided to eliminate two days because they knew students had written poems in kindergarten and first grade and were very familiar with them. Also, one of their primary goals focused on using descriptive language, and they wanted to capture as many days as possible for supporting students' word choice and figurative language. By the end of the brief discussion they felt pretty good about their decision to move two of the three days on line breaks to the section on other teaching possibilities, knowing that they could always add them back if needed.

A week later the teachers and students had started their poetry study and students had spent two days immersed in great poetry. After a minilesson about discovering topics, teachers sent students off to write their first poems of the unit. At the end of that day's workshop one of the teachers collected all of her students' poems and sat down to look at them over lunch. She quickly noticed a trend in the poems she read. While students' writing for the most part looked like poetry and included some line breaks, it didn't appear that her students were intentional in their decisions. She suspected that she would likely need more than one minilesson on line breaks, and her conferences with students after the next day's minilesson on line breaks confirmed her suspicion. In talking with her colleagues she found that several, but not all of them, had noticed the same thing. Teachers who felt their students could use the extra practice decided to reinstate the two additional days on line breaks. The trick at that point was deciding which other minilessons to take out, but this is the eternal challenge of teaching: having more to teach than available days. Collecting and surveying student writing throughout the unit helped them prioritize and make tough decisions.

As you make changes, keep notes on your unit projection template. These kinds of notes don't need to be in the reflection section. In fact, it's probably more useful to cross lessons out, right on your template, with a note to yourself about why you made the change. What you really want is to be able to look back at the end of your unit and see both what you thought you would teach and what you actually taught. This gives you a valuable starting point for the next time you teach this unit.

## Reflecting on the Unit

One of the fun parts about traveling is to sit down when it's over and look at photographs and movies from the trip. You get to relive some of your favorite sites and events. You're reminded of the things that went well (and maybe some things that didn't). You might even notice something in a photograph that you didn't pay attention to when you were there. Looking at photographs lets you slow down and reflect on the trip at your own pace.

It seems that each year teaching gets more and more rushed, contrary to what we believe is best for students. There's always another unit to squeeze in, more standards to be taught, more outcomes to be achieved. In this type of environment it easy to forget to stop and reflect on how a unit went.

Even if you've taught a unit before, we strongly encourage you to project the unit each time you teach it. Fortunately, after you've projected a unit once it's much easier to do in subsequent years. You're not starting from scratch. Rather, you're starting with last year's projection and modifying it to meet the needs of your new group of students. And, the first step in altering a unit is to pull out last year's projection sheet and look at your reflections. We encourage you to do this with another teacher or two. Here are some of the questions you might ask yourselves:

- What worked well and what didn't?
- What anticipated issues came to fruition? Which ones didn't?
- What issues arose that you didn't anticipate?
- Which goals will need to be revisited next year? Are there goals you would consider adding or deleting?
- What do you most want to remember for this unit next year?
- Which minilessons worked best?
- Which mentor texts do you definitely want to use again?
- What holes do you need to fill in your mentor text stack?

Spending a few minutes on questions like these will help you tremendously when you start the projection process for this unit next year, especially if you are forgetful, like us. Before we began recording post-unit reflections, each year when projecting a unit we had taught before we invariably would say, "There was something that didn't go well last year but I have no idea what it was." After looking at each other blankly for a few minutes we would finally give up and rationalize our memory lapse by saying, "Well, if it was really that important we would remember it, so it must not have been important." Then, of course, halfway through the unit the forgotten issue would pop up. This process helps to avoid this problem.

Here's one example. Recently we were reflecting with a group of first-grade teachers at the end of a unit called Writing All-About Books. One of the teachers said she realized that because so many of her nonfiction mentor texts had photographs rather than illustrations, her students started to think of photographs as the only way to illustrate nonfiction texts. She made a note to revise her stack to include more books with other types of illustrations the next year.

Reflecting on the unit may give you reasons to rearrange your unit order. You might decide you want to teach nonfiction early in the year because your students are really interested in it and it gives them so much energy and increases stamina right away. Or if you have struggling writers who seem to experience more success with poetry, you might decide to teach that unit early in the year to give them a sense of accomplishment.

You might even decide to do a major overhaul of the unit. Sometimes units don't go as well as planned, especially the first time you teach one (it's certainly happened to us). Reflecting on the unit now while it's fresh in your mind will be more powerful than if you wait until next year. Just because a unit didn't go well doesn't mean you have to abandon it or slog through it the same way. As you revisit your unit projection and think about next year, consider these kinds of changes:

- **Gather a different stack of mentor texts.** Perhaps the texts you selected didn't give students a clear enough vision for the type of writing they would do. Teachers are constantly adding to their stacks, and sometimes what you think is a great collection isn't the most helpful to your students. You need to see how students interact with the texts to really know if they work.

- **Spend more time on immersion.** We often find that if we don't allow time for students to really explore the stack, the unit doesn't go as well as we hoped.

- **Spend more time helping students understand the process.** Leading students through the process that an author goes through to create this type of text could be a good focus for minilessons and share time instruction.

- **Realize the first time is always a trial run.** After trying a new unit you'll understand much, much more about the unit and student writing than you did before the unit started. And now that you know more, you can make adjustments for next year.

- **Adjust your expectations.** We especially find ourselves doing this when we tackle a more challenging type of writing. We have to remember that the essays our fifth graders write in an essay unit will look like they were written by fifth graders, or that the literary nonfiction written by our first graders will look like it was made by six- and seven-year-olds.

- **Know when to let go.** While you don't want to abandon units too quickly, you might find that this unit just isn't the best one for your students. Fortunately, there is no shortage of other units of study.

We want teachers to go into units with a sense of exploration and research—let's try this out, see how it goes, and make adjustments as needed. Expecting that everything won't go as planned helps us deal with the inevitable bumps along the way. Reflection, a key part of the process, empowers you to evaluate your teaching and plan for your own growth.

In the end, you can't know what will happen. Even though you can't know exactly what each new group of students will bring to the class and exactly what they will need, you will now have a better handle on what they *might* need. You will definitely have a better idea of what published writers do well, and you will be better prepared to handle unexpected situations that arise. You will be a more responsive teacher, a teacher who watches, listens, and makes decisions based on a deeper knowledge of writing and young writers.

## PROJECTING A UNIT: Mary Alice's Realistic Fiction Unit

### Making Responsive Changes Throughout the Unit

As expected, Mary Alice's unit played out differently than she had anticipated. Figure 8.1 shows the Projected Minilesson Topics section of her projection template at the end of the unit. You can see where she noted changes and the adjustments she made as the unit progressed. Making the changes directly on the template will help her remember what occurred when she projects the unit next year. Since this book is about the process of unit projection, rather than about teaching realistic fiction, we won't give a day-by-day account of how the unit unfolded. Instead, here are several of the changes Mary Alice made that help highlight the process of making responsive decisions based on what you see with students. See Figure 8.2 for an example of a finished realistic fiction story from Mary Alice's classroom. We'll refer to it below to highlight some ways that student writing influenced her decisions.

1. After conferring with students early in the unit, Mary Alice realized that they were not consistently writing in the third person. Many introduced their characters in third person, but quickly reverted to first person. She decided to go back and revisit this. Even though this was their first attempt at writing in this genre, she wasn't comfortable with accepting an approximation from most students. She felt they could be successful with just a little more instruction. Figure 8.2 shows excerpts from a book from Mary Alice's class in which a student changed from first to third person.

2. Mary Alice realized that most students began adding dialogue to their stories right away. This may have been a result of discussions that happened during the immersion work, their familiarity with the genre, or the punctuation unit they had done earlier in the year. She decided that instead of looking at dialogue later, after some lessons about helping the reader know about the character, she would embed it earlier, within a chunk of lessons about adding details. She would now focus the lessons on using different dialogue markers, a more sophisticated technique. You can see in Figure 8.2 that the student is trying to use alternatives to the word *said*.

**Figure 8.1** Mary Alice's Projected Minilessons Section with Notes

**Projection of Possible Mini Lesson Teaching Points**

1. Immersion

2. Immersion

3. Immersion

4. Audience/purpose - celebration

5. Planning/thinking ahead – character – external and internal description

6. Planning/thinking ahead – problem and solution– keeping it real

7. Planning/thinking ahead – setting

8. Organizing – Beginning, Middle, End

9. Writing in third person  — *Need another day (having a hard time remebering to use he/she + character name*

10. Illustrations – Setting

11. Illustrations – character feelings

12. Dialogue — *already using lots - discussed words to use instead of said*

13. Character feelings - show not tell (what's in illustrations should also be in words)

14. Character feelings - internal thinking

15. Add details – blow by blow   *Add lesson on overuse of pronouns- reader confused*

16. Add detail – be specific

17. Capitalization (names)  — *Add another lesson on realistic solution*

18. Prepare for celebration – rereading and revising – more specific details  *Select text for celebration*

19. Prepare for celebration – read to partner – fluency and expression

20. Celebration

**Other Teaching Possibilities**

1. Passage of time
2. Tell rather than show
3. Interesting openings and endings
4. *When using I is okay (character dialogue + internal thought)*

**Resources/Materials/Books-** Mentor Texts, Professional Resources, etc.
Mentor Texts –
       I Want a Dog - Dayal Kaur Khalsa
       Ticky Tacky Doll – Cynthia Rylant
       Big Sister and Little Sister – Charlotte Zolotow
       Jake's 100th Day of School – Lester Laminack
       Goggles – Ezra Jack Keats
       A Letter to Amy - Ezra Jack Keats
       Peter's Chair - Ezra Jack Keats
       How to Heal a Broken Wing – Bob Graham
       "Let's Get a Pup," Said Kate – Bob Graham
       Owl Moon – Jane Yolen
Professional Resources
       First Grade Writers – Stephanie Parsons
       Study Driven – Katie Wood Ray

**Figure 8.2** First-Grade Realistic Fiction Story Excerpts

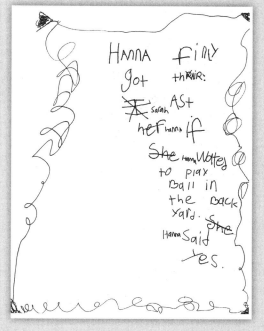

**Figure 8.2** First-Grade Realistic Fiction Story Excerpts, *cont.*

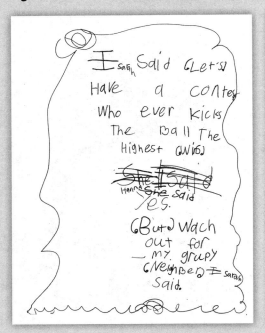

I ~~Sarah~~ Said (Let's) Have a contes who ever kicks The ball The Highest (Wins) ~~She Hanna~~ ~~She said~~ I said yes. (But) Wach out for my grupy (Neighbor) ~~I sarah~~ Said.

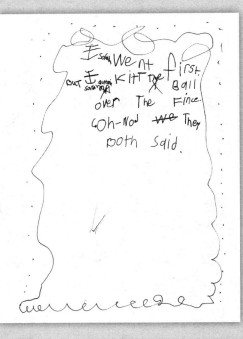

I ~~Sarah~~ ~~out I~~ ~~sarah~~ went first Kitt The ~~x~~ ball over The fince. (Oh-Now) ~~we~~ They both said.

But How will we get over The fince. ~~I don't~~ ast hanna. ~~know.~~ ~~x I have~~ I don't ~~an Idey~~ we know ~~can~~ ~~clib It~~ Replied Sarah.

I ~~Sarah~~ ~~Have~~ Has an Idey. How Bout we ues kind words. Then He won't Be so grupy.

**Figure 8.2** First-Grade Realistic Fiction Story Excerpts, *cont.*

I have better as an Idea.
We can Just CliB
it. That's a Greatz Idea.
So I (Sarah) CliBD The
Fice. and I (Sarah) Knoed
on the DOOr. and
I (Sarah) Said "Can I please
have my Ball Back."

Facts aBOut
The Auther
sarah.

my Favrit Food Is
pizza. I Am 7 years old.
I like Fashin Like
so High Heals, Facy
Dreesis, PeTy scers,
I love To WIght
Books.
"The End"

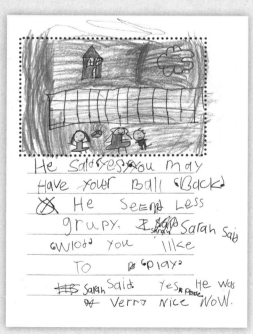

He Said Yes you may
Have your Ball Back.
He Seend Less
grupy. I (Sarah) Sarah Said
"WIod you like
To play"
Sarah Said. Yes. He was
Verra Nice WoW. "Please"

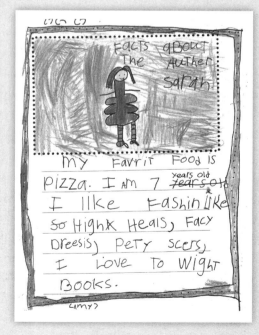

3. While listening to several partner talks, she realized she was hearing students ask each other similar questions. "Who did that?" "Who was that?" The reader was getting confused because the writer was overusing pronouns. Even the writer was often confused. Mary Alice decided she needed to add a lesson on when to use pronouns and when to use proper names.

4. Despite many conferences teaching about realistic solutions and several share times focusing on the same point, Mary Alice felt she still needed to add another lesson. Students were doing well with creating problems that could really happen but solutions seemed to move into fantasy. Because this was their first attempt at writing in this genre, she knew she needed to accept some approximations of the genre but felt by learning additional strategies the students would be able to come up with more realistic possibilities. In Figure 8.2 you can see a typical first-grade ending.

You can see that in general, Mary Alice's unit went as *projected*, but it certainly did not go exactly as planned. By reflecting on her minilessons and conferences, analyzing her conferring notes, and looking closely at students' writing in light of her primary and secondary goals, Mary Alice was able to make unit changes that responded to the needs of her students.

## Reflecting on the Unit

Soon Mary Alice and her colleagues would be projecting their next unit. But first, they spent some time reflecting on the realistic fiction unit. They wanted to make sure they remembered the specifics of how the unit went, so they wrote them in the reflection section of the template. They wanted to be able to use what they learned whenever they planned a realistic fiction unit again. You can see Mary Alice's handwritten reflections in Figure 8.3.

- Students had a high level of excitement about trying this genre.

- Focus on character in reading workshop before beginning this unit was so helpful. They quickly envisioned their own characters because of this work.

- Writing in third person was harder for them than I anticipated. I created confusion by telling them not to use the words *I* and *my*. They need to use those in dialogue and character thinking.

**Figure 8.3** Mary Alice's Unit Reflections

**Reflections**

- Students had high level of excitement about trying this genre.
- Focus on characters in Reading Workshop before beginning this unit was so helpful. They quickly envisioned their own characters because of this work
- Writing in third person was harder for them than I anticipated. I created confusion for them by telling them not to use the words I and my. They need to use those in dialogue and character thinking
- They did increase their volume of writing but seemed to have a loss of steam when getting to solution and just ended stories quickly
- More proficient writers were better benefitted from small group conferences on show not tell
- Had to remind myself this was first attempt at writing this genre especially when solutions were not really realistic

- They did increase their volume of writing but seemed to have a loss of steam when getting to the solution and just ended stories quickly.

- More proficient writers benefited from small-group conferences on show not tell.

- Had to remind myself this was a first attempt at writing this genre, especially when solutions were not really realistic.

The reflections that Mary Alice wrote will be the starting point when she plans her realistic fiction unit next year. Of course, next year's students will be different and that will impact next year's projection. But her reflections will remind her of key ideas, changes, and additions that she might forget if she didn't write them down.

## PROJECTING A UNIT IN THE INTERMEDIATE GRADES

### Making Responsive Changes Throughout the Unit

As always, the process is very similar in the intermediate grades. Here's how Mike, a fourth-grade teacher, described two of the changes he made during his realistic fiction unit.

"I had done a lot of work helping students identify character traits as they planned to write their stories, and students had written about their character in their notebooks before they started writing their drafts. I had anticipated teaching just one minilesson focused on using actions and dialogue to show character traits. A week after teaching that lesson I was reviewing my conferring notes. I noticed many of my teaching points and next steps for students indicated that most students were just telling character traits rather than using actions and dialogue. I realized that many students could identify how an author revealed traits in mentor texts, but not transfer this skill to their own writing. Based on this data, I decided to add two mini-lessons on revealing character traits: one where I showed how I do it in my writing, and one where we envisioned how students could do it in their writing and practiced it with a partner before returning to our drafts."

In Figure 8.4 you can see a writing sample from a fourth-grade class where a student is starting to reveal character traits through what the mother character in the story says about another character, Blake.

Another change Mike made involved dropped lessons. "In my original unit I had planned to teach several days on creating a setting. During the first lesson we looked at how the authors in our stack of mentor texts (short stories from children's magazines) created and let the reader know where the story was taking place. As we discussed setting it became apparent that students remembered a lot about setting from writing stories in third grade as well as from our discussions about setting in reading workshop. At the end of writing workshop that day I asked students to leave their writing out so I could look at it while they were at lunch. During lunch I did a quick survey. In almost all of their stories I could quickly tell where their stories were taking place, and many of the students were embedding their settings skillfully in their stories. I decided that I didn't need additional days on setting and would instead pull together a few students who needed additional practice creating settings as a small-group conference the next day."

In Figure 8.5 we can see evidence of a student embedding setting.

**Figure 8.4** Student Reveals Character Traits Through Dialogue

# My Friend's Lost Toy!

"My friend Kevin let me borrow his new toy," Blake said to his mom. His mother replied, "Take care of it, Blake. I know how forgetful you are." Blake started to play with it. He played so long he didn't realize it was now dark outside. His mom came in his room and said, "Blake, time for bed." "Awe," answered Blake. So he carelessly put down the toy in his messy room overflowing with other toys.

It became morning and Blake asked, "What are we having for breakfast?" "Eggs and bacon," answered mom." "Hey Blake, when is Kevin going to be here to pick up his toy?" asked his mom. "I don't know, but I'm going to go play with it right now."

So Blake went to his room to play with Kevin's new toy except Blake could not find it. "Where is it?" Blake shouted. Mom came in and asked, "What is wrong?" "I can not find Kevin's new toy." Mom replied, "It is probably in your messy room."

That's when Blake frantically started to clean his messy room. "Mom I still can't find it." So his mom helped him until they heard the sound of knocking on the door. "Who is that at the door?" "I will go see," said Blake. "Its Kevin." "Oh no what am I going to do" thought Blake. "Can I please play with it for two more hours?" begged Blake. "Sure," answered Kevin. "Thanks," replied Blake.

He continued to clean his room for the next hour and fifty-five minutes. Blake was beginning to think he would never find it. He was starting to sweat when… "Mom look! I found it!" yelled Blake. "Where was it" asked mom. "I only have five minutes. I'm going to clean up the toy. It was covered in the juice I spilled *last month*." muttered Blake sadly.

Just then there was a knocking at the door. Blake answered the door. Kevin asked Blake for his new toy. So Blake happily gave it back to Kevin and said "I never want to see that toy again!"

**By Christopher**

**"I lost Kevin's toy!"**

## Reflecting on the Unit

Once again the process is very similar in the intermediate grades. While the content of the reflections might be different since different content was taught, the importance of taking time to reflect on how the unit unfolded, what went well, what changes were made, and what you want to be sure to remember for next year is the same.

**Figure 8.5** Student Embeds Setting

One afternoon Sydney Browne looked out the window and that's when it all started. "Hey look Anna, there is a new girl moving in across the street", said Sydney. "Where?" said Anna, as she ran into her little sister Sydney's room. She curled up around Sydney as they peered out the window together. "Right there", said Sydney, as she pointed to the girl riding her bike. With excitement, the girl's jumped off the bed, eager to meet the neighbor.

The girl's sped over on their bikes to meet the new girl. As they approached the new neighbor's driveway the girl shyly waved. Anna and Sydney introduced themselves to the new girl. The new girl replied "Hi, my name is Mary." Anna and Sydney were not focusing on Mary, but on the training wheels she had attached to her bike. The girls didn't mean to stare. They thought it was awkward that a seven year old would still need training wheels. Anna and Sydney's mother called them in for dinner. The girl's told each other goodbye. As the Browne girl's rode up their driveway, Sydney whispered to Anna, "do you like her...I don't like her because she still has training wheels on her bike." "Yes it is a little babyish."

Eight o'clock Saturday morning, Mary flew down her driveway, on her bike, ready to play. "Come back here!" shouted Mary's mom. "It is too early to knock on the Browne's door, they are probably still asleep." Mary shouted back to her mother "ok, but I still want to ride. I promise I will not knock on the Browne's door." Off Mary went on her bike to explore the neighborhood.

Mary found something very interesting. There standing in front of her was a huge Live Oak tree with a wooden swing hanging from it's branches. As Mary got closer she realized there were carvings on the tree. It read *Anna and Sydney.* Mary wondered if she could carve her name in the tree. She thought for a moment and decided she should ask Anna and Sydney first before she carved her name. She hopped on her bike and raced home to ask her mom if she could knock on the Browne's door. "Yes you may, but be polite." Mary couldn't wait to tell the girls what she had discovered.

Mary ran up the steps to the Browne's front door and was out of breath from excitement. She rang the bell and Sydney answered. "I have something to ask you!" said Mary. "I found the tree that you and your sister carved your names into." Sydney said "Oh yeah that tree." Mary asked if she could also carve her name in the tree. Sydney was quiet for a moment before she answered Mary's question. Sydney let out a large sigh and then called Anna to the front door. Sydney gently shut the front door so that she could talk to Anna in private. They decided together that they did not want Mary to sign the tree, because she was seven and still had training wheels. After a couple of minutes the girl's opened the door and broke the disappointing news to Mary. Mary shed a tear and went home with her head hung low.

Sydney had trouble sleeping that night. The only thing she could think of was how badly she hurt Mary's feelings. She tossed and turned all night and imagined herself in Mary's shoes. She couldn't believe what she had done. Sydney wished that she could have taken it back.

The next morning Sydney knew just what she needed to do. Right after breakfast she rushed into Anna's room to tell her how miserable she felt for treating Mary so rudely. Anna felt badly as well. They both walked over to Mary's to apologize with the special tree carving stick. Mary's mom answered the door. She greeted Sydney and Anna with a cheerful smile. Sydney and Anna asked if they could speak to Mary. Mary heard the girl's and poked her head out from behind the front door. "We are so sorry for judging your ability to ride your bike. We should treat you the way we want to be treated. The "Golden Rule" is so important to remember. We have something special we want to do with you" said Sydney. Mary said "What is that?" "Come along and you will see" said Anna. The girl's took Mary by the hand and led her to the Live Oak tree. They handed Mary the special carving stick. She wrote *Mary.* From that moment forward the three girls were best friends. Sydney and Anna taught Mary how to ride a bike without training wheels!

Sydney and Anna never judged people again!

*The End!*

**Try It Out**

At the end of the unit spend a few minutes reflecting on the unit. You might ask yourself these questions.

1. What worked well and what didn't?

2. What anticipated issues came to fruition? Which ones didn't?

3. What issues arose that you didn't anticipate?

4. Which goals will need to be revisited next year? Are there goals you would consider adding or deleting?

5. What do you most want to remember for this unit next year?

6. Which minilessons worked best?

7. Which mentor texts do you definitely want to use again?

8. What holes do you need to fill in your mentor text stack?

# Conclusion

Several years ago, two teachers transferred to the school where Matt and Mary Alice were working. After a couple of months, Matt asked them how things were going. They replied enthusiastically, "Great. This year we get to think!" They went on to explain that at their previous school, lessons were planned for them and the expectation was that every teacher in the grade level would be teaching the same lesson at the same time. They weren't asked to think about what to teach, because someone else had done it for them.

There are two big advantages to the idea of encouraging and expecting teachers to make decisions about what to teach in a unit of study. Perhaps most obviously, when teachers make the decisions, instruction meets the particular needs of students. In their previous school experience, these two teachers had become frustrated when day-by-day writing plans didn't reflect the needs of the students in front of them. They *wanted* to be encouraged to think and make responsive decisions that would genuinely help each of their students learn.

The second advantage is that as you become more responsive to student's needs by thinking about curriculum and projecting units yourselves, you learn much more about the craft of writing. Your knowledge base about particular genres is enriched and you understand writing processes in a deeper way. You also learn to think through potential sequences of learning. The current environment of increasing standards makes it even more important that teachers be encouraged to understand not only what needs to be learned, but to think creatively about how to get there.

We can't know what impact this book will have, but we have several hopes. We hope that the process for projecting a unit of study provides you with strategies for better understanding the teaching of writing. We hope this book supports you in interpreting standards and making decisions based on the needs of your students. By increasing your knowledge about the type of writing required in any unit, we hope it is easier for you to make decisions about what to teach in whole-group, small-group, and one-on-one situations that respond to the individual needs of the learners you work with each day.

We hope that understanding both the need for projecting a unit and the projecting process will impact your teaching outside of writing workshop as well. The advantages for projecting your teaching are the same regardless of the content area. The basic process for projecting a unit—studying the content, setting goals, projecting learning experiences, and making responsive decisions along the way—is similar for whatever subject you are teaching.

Most of all, we hope you are excited to gather a group of colleagues and a stack of texts, and project a unit together. We hope that thinking deeply about what to teach in writing workshop will ensure that the units you create foster deeper learning, both for you and for your students.

# Appendix

## Possible Units of Study

There are myriad possible units to study in writing workshop, and many resources provide support for teachers as they project a unit of study. The purpose of this appendix is to open up the range of units. We've decided to organize these units by resources that examine particular units of study to make it easy to find out more about them. Our hope is that seeing the wide range of potential units will expand the possibilities for your class.

**About the Authors by Katie Wood Ray—Primary Grades**

- The Kinds of Things Writers Make and How We'll Make Them in This Room
- Where Writers Get Ideas
- How to Read Like Writers
- Finding Writing Mentors
- How to Structure Text in Interesting Ways
- How to Make Illustrations Work Better with Written Text
- How to Have Better Peer Conferences
- Literary Nonfiction
- How Authors Use Punctuation in Interesting Ways
- Poetry
- Revision

**Study Driven** by Katie Wood Ray

- Memoir
- Short Stories of Realistic Fiction
- Historical Fiction
- True Stories from History: Historical Narrative
- Crafting Family Stories into Literature
- Poetry
- Journeys of Thought: The Essay
- Feature Articles and Literary Nonfiction
- Practical How-To Writing
- Informative How-To Writing
- Advice Writing
- Feature Articles Based on Interviews
- Exploring Possibilities: List Articles
- Biographical Sketches and Profiles
- Editorials, Commentary, and All Things Op-Ed
- ABC Texts
- Reviews
- News Reporting
- Photo Essay
- Slice of Life Writing
- Topical Writing
- Survey of Different Kinds of Writing in the World
- Multigenre Writing
- How Writers Use Punctuation as a Crafting Tool
- How Illustrations and Graphics Enhance Meaning
- How Writers Make Paragraphing Decisions
- How Writers Craft Texts in Interesting Ways
- How to Craft Using Obvious Text Structures
- The Work of Authors' Notes in Texts
- How Writers Decide on Titles

***Engaging Young Writers* by Matt Glover—Primary Grades (non-genre-specific units that could come at the beginning of the year)**

- Launching Book Making in the Writing Workshop
- Where Writers Get Ideas
- Drawing for Meaning/Illustration Study
- Reading Like a Writer
- Genre Overview Study

***Units of Study Grades K–2* by Lucy Calkins**

- Launching the Writing Workshop
- Small Moments: Personal Narrative Writing
- Writing for Readers: Teaching Skills and Strategies
- The Craft of Revision
- Authors as Mentors
- Nonfiction Writing: Procedures and Reports
- Poetry: Powerful Thoughts in Tiny Packages

***Units of Study Grades 3–5* by Lucy Calkins**

- Launching the Writing Workshop
- Raising the Quality of Narrative Writing
- Breathing Life into Essays
- Story Arcs: Writing Short Fiction
- Writing About Literature
- Memoir: Putting It All Together

**Units of Study Described in *Of Primary Importance* by Ann Marie Corgill—Primary Grades**

- From Ordinary to Extraordinary: Teaching and Learning About Poetry with Primary Writers
- Inquiring Minds Want to Know: Teaching and Learning About Nonfiction Writing with Primary Writers
- Picture This: Teaching and Learning About Picture Books with Primary Writers

***Significant Studies for Second-Grade Reading and Writing Investigations for Children* by Karen Ruzzo and Mary Anne Sacco**

- Getting Started in the Writing Workshop: Writing About Memories, Introducing Picture Books, and Experimenting with Forms and Techniques
- Creating Setting in Writing
- Content Area Research and Writing

***First Grade Writers* by Stephanie Parsons**

- Building a Community of Writers
- Pattern Books
- Nonfiction Question and Answer Books
- Personal Narrative
- Fiction

***Second Grade Writers* by Stephanie Parsons**

- Becoming a Community of Writers
- Writing for Change
- Writing a Book Review
- Exploring Humor
- Writing About Research

**Resources for a Single Unit of Study**

Illustration Study: *In Pictures and In Words* by Katie Wood Ray

Memoir: *Writing a Life* by Katherine Bomer

Poetry: *Awakening the Heart: Exploring Poetry in the Elementary and Middle Grades* by Georgia Heard

Poetry: *Kids' Poems* series by Regie Routman

Persuasive Writing (various units): *Writing to Persuade* by Karen Caine

Nonfiction Writing: *Is That a Fact?* by Tony Stead

Fiction: *Making Believe on Paper: Fiction Writing with Young Children* by Ted  DeMille

# Appendix  B

## Units of Study Projection Template

Unit of Study: _____

_____ Genre Specific _____ Non-Genre Specific _____ # of Weeks

**Primary Goals:**

1.

2.

3.

**Secondary Goals: Writing Quality, Writing Habits, Revision, Community of Writers, Editing/Conventions**

1.

2.

3.

4.

5.

6.

**Anticipated Issues:**

1.

2.

**Projection of Possible Mini Lesson Topics:**

1.

2.

3.

**4.**

**5.**

**6.**

**7.**

**8.**

**9.**

**10.**

**11.**

**12.**

**13.**

**14.**

**15.**

**16.**

**17.**

**18.**

**19.**

**20.**

**Other Teaching Possibilities:**

**1.**

**Resources/Materials/Books:** Mentor texts, professional resources, etc.

**Reflections:**

# Appendix

## Critical and Possible Units of Study

**Grade Level** _____

| Critical Units | Possible Units |
|---|---|
| | |

# Appendix  D

## Resources for Understanding
## the Qualities of Good Writing

The more you know about the qualities of good writing, the bigger pool of possible teaching points you'll have for minilessons and conferences. These resources can help.

*Assessing Writers* by Carl Anderson

*Strategic Writing Conferences: Smart Conversations That Move Young Writers Forward* by Carl Anderson

*The Art of Teaching Writing*, 2nd edition, by Lucy Calkins

*6 + 1 Traits of Writing* by Ruth Culham

*Teaching the Qualities of Writing, Grades 3–6* by Ralph Fletcher and Joan Portalupi

*Mentor Author, Mentor Texts: Short Texts, Craft Notes, and Practical Classroom Uses* by Ralph Fletcher

*What a Writer Needs* by Ralph Fletcher

*Craft Lessons* by Ralph Fletcher and Joanne Portalupi

*Cracking Open the Author's Craft: Teaching the Art of Writing* by Lester Laminack

*In Pictures and in Words* by Katie Wood Ray

*Wondrous Words* by Katie Wood Ray

*What You Know by Heart: How to Develop Curriculum for Your Writing Workshop* by Katie Wood Ray

*The Writing Workshop: Working Through the Hard Parts* by Katie Wood Ray and Lester Laminack

# Appendix  E

## Resources for Reading Like a Writer

The ability to read like a writer is fundamental for students to learn to write well. Here are a few of the resources that can help teachers learn more about this crucial skill.

*The Art of Teaching Writing* by Lucy Calkins

*Mentor Author, Mentor Texts: Short Texts, Craft Notes, and Practical Classroom Uses* by Ralph Fletcher

*Cracking Open the Author's Craft: Teaching the Art of Writing* by Lester Laminack

*Wondrous Words* by Katie Wood Ray

*What You Know by Heart* by Katie Wood Ray

*Already Ready* by Katie Wood Ray and Matt Glover

*Study Driven* by Katie Wood Ray

*The Writing Workshop: Working Through the Hard Parts* by Katie Wood Ray and Lester Laminack

*Joining the Literacy Club* by Frank Smith

# Appendix

## Celebrations

The celebration is intended not just to recognize the hard work of the students, although that certainly is something to celebrate. More importantly, it gives students a reason to write. It creates a purpose for the writing. It gives them real reasons to revise and edit. And when we say think about your reader, they know there really will be a reader!

In school celebrations:

Invite people into your classroom to hear your students read their work. Students can be grouped in different ways—small groups reading to an adult, one on one with another student, and so on.

Some people you might consider inviting:

- Other classes in your school
- Adults in the building, including administrators, fine arts teachers, office staff, cafeteria and custodial staff
- Parents and families
- Bus drivers
- Students in our class—we often forget to give them the opportunity to share finished products with each other

Send writing out into the world:

- Place books in the school or public library to be read by others. Attach a comment sheet so people can leave a message for the child.
- Place books out in the community—doctor and dentist offices, Chamber of Commerce office, and other visible locations.
- Post student writing on a classroom blog.

# Children's Books Cited

Bansch, H. 2009. *I Want a Dog*. New York: North-South Books.

Catalanato, P. 1989. *Dylan's Day Out*. New York: Orchard Books.

Davies, N. 2001. *Bat Loves the Night*. Cambridge, MA: Candlewick Press.

Fletcher, R. 2005. *Marshfield Dreams*. New York: Henry Holt.

Frazee, M. 2003. *Roller Coaster*. New York: Harcourt.

Graham, B. 2008. *How to Heal a Broken Wing*. Somerville, MA: Candlewick Press.

———. 2010. *"The Trouble with Dogs . . . " Said Dad*. Somerville, MA: Candlewick Press.

Henkes, K. 1991. *Chrysanthemum*. New York: Greenwillow Books.

———. 2000. *Wemberly Worried*. New York: Greenwillow Books.

———. 2005. *Lily's Purple Plastic Purse*. New York: Greenwillow Books.

Keats, E. 1998. *Peter's Chair*. New York: Puffin Books.

———. 1998. *Goggles*. New York: Puffin Books.

Paul, C. 2009. *Long Shot*. New York: Simon & Schuster.

Pilkey, Dav. 1999. *The Paperboy*. New York: Scholastic.

Raschka, C. 1993. *Yo! Yes?* New York: Scholastic.

Rylant, C. 2002. *The Ticky Tacky Doll*. New York: Harcourt.

Spinelli, E. 2001. *In My New Yellow Shirt*. New York: Henry Holt.

Vaccaro Seeger, L. 2007. *Dog and Bear: Two Friends, Three Stories*. New York: Roaring Brook Press.

Waddell, M. 1992. *Owl Babies*. Cambridge, MA: Candlewick Press.

Yolen, J. 1987. *Owl Moon*. New York: Philomel Books.

———. 2003. *Hoptoad*. New York: Harcourt.

# Bibliography

Anderson, C. 2000. *How's It Going: A Practical Guide to Conferring with Student Writers.* Portsmouth, NH: Heinemann.

_____. 2005. *Assessing Writers.* Portsmouth, NH: Heinemann.

_____. 2009. *Strategic Writing Conferences: Smart Conversations That Move Young Writers Forward.* Portsmouth, NH: Heinemann.

Bomer, K. 2005. *Writing a Life: Teaching Memoir to Sharpen Insight, Shape Meaning—and Triumph Over Tests.* Portsmouth, NH: Heinemann.

_____. 2010. *Hidden Gems: Naming and Teaching from the Brilliance in Every Student's Writing.* Portsmouth, NH: Heinemann.

Caine, K. 2008. *Writing to Persuade: Minilessons to Help Students Plan, Draft, and Revise, Grades 3–8.* Portsmouth, NH: Heinemann.

Calkins, L. 2001. *The Art of Teaching Writing.* New York: Addison-Wesley.

_____. 2003. *Units of Study for Primary Writing: A Yearlong Curriculum K–2.* Portsmouth, NH: Heinemann.

_____. 2006. *Units of Study for Teaching Writing, Grades 3–5.* Portsmouth, NH: Heinemann.

_____. 2006. *Memoir: The Art of Writing Well.* Portsmouth, NH: Heinemann.

Corgill, A.M. 2008. *Of Primary Importance: What's Essential in Teaching Young Writers.* Portland, ME: Stenhouse.

Culham, R. 2003. *6 + 1 Traits of Writing: The Complete Guides Grade 3 and Up.* New York: Scholastic.

DeMille, T. 2008. *Making Believe on Paper: Fiction Writing with Young Children.* Portsmouth, NH: Heinemann.

Edwards, C., L. Gandini, and G. Forman, eds. 1998. *The Hundred Languages of Children 2nd Edition.* Norwood, NJ: Ablex.

Fletcher, R. 1992. *What a Writer Needs.* Portsmouth, NH: Heinemann.

_____. 2011. *Mentor Author, Mentor Texts: Short Texts, Craft Notes, and Practical Classroom Uses.* Portsmouth, NH: Heinemann.

Fletcher, R. and J. Portalupi. 2004. *Teaching the Qualities of Writing, Grades 3–6.* Portsmouth, NH: Heinemann.

_____. 2007. *Craft Lessons: Teaching Writing K–8 (2nd Ed.).* Portland, ME: Stenhouse.

Glover, M. 2009. *Engaging Young Writers, Preschool–Grade One.* Portsmouth, NH: Heinemann.

Heard, G. 1998. *Awakening the Heart: Exploring Poetry in Elementary and Middle School.* Portsmouth, NH: Heinemann.

Laminack, L. 2007. *Cracking Open the Author's Craft: Teaching the Art of Writing.* New York: Scholastic.

Newkirk, T. 2009. "Stress, Control, and the Deprofessionalizing of Teachers." *Education Week* 29, 24–25.

Parsons, S. 2005. *First Grade Writers: Units of Study to Help Children Plan, Organize, and Structure Their Ideas.* Portsmouth, NH: Heinemann.

_____. 2007. *Second Grade Writers: Units of Study to Help Children Focus on Audience and Purpose.* Portsmouth, NH: Heinemann.

Parsons, S. Interview by author, July 2011.

Ray, K. 1999. *Wondrous Words: Writers and Writing in the Elementary Classroom.* Urbana, IL: NCTE.

_____. 2002. *What You Know by Heart: How to Develop Curriculum for Your Writing Workshop.* Portsmouth, NH: Heinemann.

_____. 2006. *Study Driven: A Framework for Planning Units of Study in the Writing Workshop.* Portsmouth, NH: Heinemann.

_____. 2010. *In Pictures and in Words: Teaching the Qualities of Good Writing Through Illustration Study.* Portsmouth, NH: Heinemann.

Ray, K. Email to Matt Glover, September 11, 2011.

Ray, K., with L. Cleaveland. 2004. *About the Authors: Writing Workshop with Our Youngest Writers.* Portsmouth, NH: Heinemann.

Ray, K., with L. Laminack. 2001. *The Writing Workshop: Working Through the Hard Parts (and They're All Hard Parts).* Urbana, IL: NCTE.

Ray, K., and M. Glover. 2008. *Already Ready: Nurturing Young Writers in Preschool and Kindergarten.* Portsmouth, NH: Heinemann.

Routman, R. 2000. *Kids Poems Series.* New York: Scholastic.

Ruzzo, K., and Sacco, M.A. 2004. *Significant Studies for Second Grade: Reading and Writing Investigations for Children:* Portsmouth, NH: Heinemann.

Smith, F. 1987. *Joining the Literacy Club: Further Essays into Education.* Portsmouth, NH: Heinemann.

Stead, T. 2001. *Is That a Fact: Teaching Nonfiction Writing K–3.* Portland, ME: Stenhouse.

Wilson, M. 2006. *Rethinking Rubrics in Writing Assessment.* Portsmouth, NH: Heinemann.

# About the Authors

Over more than 15 years of collaboration, **MATT GLOVER** and **MARY ALICE BERRY** have shared a passion for fostering writers' growth. They know this can't be achieved in a one-size-fits-all curriculum. Their deep experience shows through in *Projecting Possibilities for Writers*, helping you design writing experiences that engage students and empower teacher decision making.

**MATT GLOVER** is a full time educational consultant and author. He is the author of the Heinemann title *Engaging Young Writers* and coauthor with Katie Wood Ray of *Already Ready* and *Watch Katie and Matt...Sit Down and Teach Up*, a video enhanced ebook that combines video and text to examine conferring with young writers. A nationally known literacy consultant, Matt is a frequent presenter at conferences and in school districts on topics related to nurturing writers and supporting children's intellectual growth and development. Matt has been an educator for over 20 years, including 12 years as the principal and instructional leader of Creekside Early Childhood School. Matt lives in Cincinnati, OH with his wife and four children.

**MARY ALICE BERRY** is an experienced early childhood educator with thirty-four years experience. She has worked as a literacy specialist, media specialist, and instructional leader. Currently she is a first grade teacher at Shawnee Early Childhood School in West Chester, Ohio. Inside the classroom, Mary Alice's work focuses on developmentally appropriate practices that foster the intellectual as well as the academic growth of students. Outside, she conducts many literacy workshops and lives in Trenton, Ohio with her husband and two dogs.

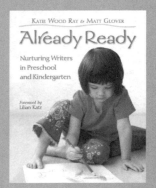